what
girls
need

what girls need

How to Raise Bold, Courageous and Resilient Women

Marisa Porges, PhD

Vermilion
LONDON

1

Vermilion, an imprint of Ebury Publishing
20 Vauxhall Bridge Road,
London SW1V 2SA

Vermilion is part of the Penguin Random House group of companies
whose addresses can be found at global.penguinrandomhouse.com

Penguin
Random House
UK

First published in the United Kingdom in 2020 by Vermilion
First published in the United States in 2020 by Viking, an imprint of Penguin
Random House LLC, New York

www.penguin.co.uk

A CIP catalogue record for this book is available from the British Library

ISBN 9781785042805

Printed and bound in Great Britain by Clays Ltd, Elcograf S.p.A.

Penguin Random House is committed to a sustainable
future for our business, our readers and our planet.
This book is made from Forest Stewardship Council®
certified paper.

For Scott,
what every girl needs
in a partner and best friend

Contents

Author's Note

What Girls Need

I vividly remember the first time I lost my voice—not my actual voice, but the ability to speak my mind and stand my ground.

I was a second-year student in college, in the midst of summer training for the U.S. military. With the stubborn confidence of a nineteen-year-old, I delighted in wearing a borrowed flight suit to work each day and doing odd jobs at a naval aviation squadron in Jacksonville, Florida. Even as a glorified intern, I'd call my parents to breathlessly share stories of what life was like as a naval aviator. I pictured childhood dreams of life as a fighter jet pilot coming true and imagined how things would unfold from there. It was going just as I'd hoped until the sticky summer day when a senior officer, a trained Navy pilot with years of experience and expertise, pulled me aside in the squadron ready room and sneeringly told me that naval aviation wasn't for me. That I'd never cut it as an aviator "because I was a girl".

The slap of those words stings to this day. What's worse, I

still cringe when I recall my muted response. I didn't know what to say or how to respond. I was at a loss for how to stand up for myself.

When I remember this moment and the feeling of being unfairly attacked and left reeling, unprepared to advocate for myself, it's hard not to let my mind spiral to other painful memories. I wince when I recall that I failed at negotiating because I didn't know how to ask effectively. Or when I think of that coveted job I didn't get because I didn't even compete for the opportunity. Then there were the missed chances to network in a room full of men, when I underrated my natural ability to develop relationships and connect with others in a uniquely personal, empathetic way. Like many women, I keep a neatly organized and overstuffed mental file of these moments and more—all the times when subtly, often unconsciously, and always regrettably, I sensed that "because I'm a girl" held me back rather than served as my competitive edge.

Looking back on these and other moments involves a mix of regret and embarrassment, but also quiet gratitude—gratitude because over time these missteps taught me critical lessons about how to navigate the real world. These are lessons that I didn't get when I was young but that made all the difference later on, personally and professionally. Lessons that eventually helped me realize my dream of flying jets off aircraft carriers despite being too short to see over the jet's dashboard, too light for the ejection seat, and typically the token girl in a roomful of men.

Now I can see that my moments of failure and success taught me as much as the lessons my parents, teachers, and mentors intentionally crafted for me, and honed critical life skills that

Author's Note

I've relied on ever since. These experiences helped me to survive wandering through southern Afghanistan, conducting interviews with former Taliban and local tribal leaders during the height of fighting season, despite traveling solo, with no security detail by my side or weapon in my handbag, and being one of the only Jewish American women my Afghan contacts had ever met. The skills I gained over the years also helped me navigate the politics of the White House and the drama of the Pentagon, where I shaped U.S. counterterrorism and cybersecurity efforts under two presidents, despite constantly being aware of the length of my hair (a male colleague had advised me to keep it long), of the style of my clothes (another had told me to be mindful of wearing stylish high boots to work), and of the fact that I was making less money than my male peers (again, the result of my poor negotiating skills). All of these life lessons now guide my daily work, helping me give the nearly six hundred young girls at my school what they need to succeed, in class and in life.

As the head of the Baldwin School in the suburbs of Philadelphia, I lead a 130-year-old all-girls school for students from reception to the end of secondary school. Baldwin was founded on the premise that an education specially tailored to young women can propel them to break barriers in a male-dominated world. I spend every day thinking about what works and what doesn't for girls and partnering with parents and teachers to understand the dynamics at play for young women, socially and emotionally. Because Baldwin is a school known for challenging girls academically and shaping them as future leaders, we focus on providing girls with specific tools to ensure they succeed after graduation, in any and every environment. And we don't ignore the fact that all of our girls are likely to face major hurdles in life specifically because they're women—and that we must teach them early on how to meet these challenges head-on and how to take advantage of the innate talents that set them apart.

Not because girls need to be more like boys, or women more like men, in spite of the clichés about a woman needing to behave like a man to excel in a "man's world". But as gender dynamics slowly and finally evolve, we need to think differently about how we prepare our girls to be the leaders, innovators, and game-changers they dream of becoming. Every girl should learn skills early on that empower her to be her best self. So that our girls grow into women able to apply grit, confidence, and bravery in real-world situations and effectively advocate for themselves. So that our daughters have the skills needed not just to compete with men but to turn their intrinsic talents into competitive advantages. So that our girls create their own success, no matter what the future holds and whatever comes their way.

What Girls Need describes what is essential for every young girl to learn early on and outlines how parents, teachers, friends, and family can help young girls develop the skills they need to become not just self-assured but feisty, too. Not just brave but bold. Not just confident but audacious. The chapters that follow use social science research, case studies, and examples from around the world, as well as personal stories from my time flying for the U.S. Navy, working in the White House, and traveling through the Middle East, to describe what we can do for girls to give them an edge as adult women. That way they can thrive, personally and professionally, even in the face of gender-based discrimination and sexual harassment.

The girls I work with each day are examples of why these lessons are so critical for today's young women. They are fortunate to have one of the best educations in the nation at their fingertips, and I'm constantly impressed by how hard they work and how talented they are. But they are still concerned about what's to come and how they will handle the fast-changing and unknown future. Their parents are worried, too. They fear that their girls' confidence won't matter the first time they are spoken over—or down to—at a meeting, despite being expert in whatever is being discussed. They are concerned that all the resilience in the world won't matter when their daughter's first boss makes a pass at them. They fear that their girls won't be fully prepared to successfully navigate and feel empowered in the twenty-first-century world, and that no matter how much education and training they provide, their little girls might not be ready for the gender bias that still pervades society.

As I speak to anxious parents, I constantly hear about the onslaught of public reporting on sexual harassment in the workplace and sexual violence on college campuses. Mums who deal with gender discrimination at work worry about what it will be like for their daughters. Dads are apprehensive about what sort of world their daughters will enter when they grow up and leave home.

So I wasn't surprised to hear Marc, the father of two girls, Carrie and Amanda, describe having daughters as the best and worst thing ever. "I think they're both perfect, each in her own special way. They're the favourite parts of my day," Marc says. "But the second thought that goes through my head—that goes through the mind of any father of girls—is 'Wow, do they have a tough road ahead...' It's terrifying when you stop to think about it."

Over the course of multiple conversations, Marc and I discussed whether his girls' education equipped them for life. Were they prepared for college, where approximately 23 per cent of young women are raped or sexually assaulted, and two-thirds experience sexual harassment? Were they ready for the working world, where 42 per cent of women face discrimination because of their gender, and where approximately 25 per cent earn less than a man doing the same job?

What stuck out most was Marc's memory from Amanda's final year at Baldwin. "We were wading through the normal muck that is a Tuesday in our house, and she came to me with some dire problem. Something to do with her singing group. I can't even recall now what happened, except that she and her friends were upset and thought the teacher and school were in the wrong."

"What did you do?" I asked.

"I went into dad mode, of course," Marc admitted sheepishly. "I asked whether I should call the school or talk to the teacher."

"And..." I pressed, curious to know what happened next and hoping that Amanda responded as the independent, resilient girl I knew her to be—as the young woman who knew how to effectively advocate for herself, even at seventeen years old.

"She was horrified! Told me not to get involved and was a bit embarrassed, for me I think, that I'd even suggest such a thing."

I was relieved and also proud to hear proof that Marc's

daughter Amanda was prepared—because she was strong enough to speak up for herself, to take action when needed, and to find her voice when faced with a challenge. Because she learned these key lessons early on, I was certain she could boldly be her best self and apply her innate talents to maximum effect.

At Baldwin, we want every young girl to grow into an Amanda. Or into Sabrina, an audacious Year 7 pupil who scheduled an appointment with me soon after I became head of school to formally propose a standing advisory committee of middle school pupils who'd help me run the school and make major decisions. I let my board of trustees know they had some competition from our twelve-year-olds.

My work before Baldwin could serve as a personal narrative of this book's lessons, illustrating why women need special skills to succeed and what happens when we don't teach girls these lessons early on. From my service on active duty in the U.S. Navy to my work as a counterterrorism scholar and national security advisor, I know first-hand why the conversation about *What Girls Need* is long overdue.

I wasn't prepared for the moments when I discovered that even in the twenty-first century, my gender could still hold me back. These are the scenes that hit me like a slap in the face and remain seared in my memory. Like when a supervisor entered my squadron ready room, looked me up and down, and loudly complimented me on how well my flight suit fit my curves. Or when I led a delegation of U.S. officials to the Middle East and our Kuwaiti government counterpart refused to deal with me, wondering aloud when a man would arrive to represent America.

Author's Note

Or when, one bitterly cold night in southern Afghanistan, a senior military officer knocked on the door of my cramped sleeping quarters thinking that our mentor–mentee relationship would no doubt mean a sexual relationship, too.

I was only partially prepared. More could have been done for me and my female friends and colleagues when we were girls and young women to make sure we didn't just survive but thrived as adults, in our careers and beyond. Because while lessons from when I was young taught me the value of confidence and resilience, the need to be a creative thinker and a hard worker, it took me years to appreciate the role that self-advocating, negotiating, and competing, among other skills, play in the real world. What's more, it wasn't until recently that I understood the influence of the innate talents many women have, including the ability to problem-solve collaboratively, connect and communicate across boundaries, and employ empathy to maximum effect. These skills could be our girls' competitive advantage, no matter what challenge is headed their way or where the twenty-first century leads them in the decades to come.

Imagine if we started teaching these lessons early on? Rather than waiting until young women are entering the workforce, what if we help school-aged girls grow comfortable with these skills and talents from an early age so they begin to embrace them naturally? So these traits become tools to employ organically as they grow up?

With this vision in mind, I recall the counterterrorism research I conducted in Yemen and Saudi Arabia with a new perspective. I was lucky to turn the disadvantage of being a solo

Author's Note

American female traveling in the region on its head—because I was able to empathize with locals I met along the way. Because I could connect with them in ways that many people—especially, according to social science research, my male colleagues—find difficult. I still remember the powerful feeling of exploring a souk in the Old City of Sana'a, dressed in a Yemeni abaya, and being invited to share meals with local families in their homes, where I met their children and heard stories that they'd not so readily share with an American man.

When I look back on this time, I now see that an ability to empathize authentically with those who crossed my path made the biggest difference and helped me use my gender to competitive advantage. It's why, when a Saudi friend talked about how he thought I was different from the Americans he knew, it was a compliment. He was comparing me to guys he knew and, in gentlemanly albeit broken English, affirming the powerful distinction that was my feminine advantage. Even in Saudi society, well known for its gender bias.

With this vision in mind, I remember in a new way my second year at Harvard, when I found myself in a compromising situation with a final-year student—a cute, charming senior who seemed so interesting after a few drinks at an off-campus party. The sort of boy I imagined would be nice on a date and might even make a good boyfriend.

I didn't credit my ability to self-advocate when, despite a mind dulled from alcohol, I heard alarm bells go off in the back of my mind after he brought me to his dorm. I didn't realize I was boldly using my voice when I asked him to slow down. I didn't know I had the skills that mattered most when I said that I didn't want to have sex. All I recall is being unceremoniously shown the dorm-room door in the middle of the night. Instead of being proud, I was embarrassed—and then grateful when a friend spotted me crying in the street and escorted me home.

With this vision in mind, I think again about countless moments when things worked out—or didn't—and appreciate that the key ingredient in my success wasn't confidence or resilience, education or courage. What mattered most was how I could pair those elements with specific skills and talents that became personal strengths—everything from self-advocacy and the willingness to compete to the ability to lead teams in problem-solving and empathize with those different from me in every way possible. That's what girls need, now and for the future.

In the chapters ahead, we will explore together these concepts and discuss how to help your girl find her voice, nurture her competitive spirit, turn her audacity into persuasiveness, and leverage her innate talents for problem-solving, empathizing, and adapting. All these are skills and ways of being that will help her succeed as an adult woman in the decades ahead. Along the way, I'll also explore what little things make a big difference in empowering our girls, so that they learn to deal with the disapproving looks, snarky comments, and occasional censure that can come with being an audacious woman.

You don't have to be a feminist to care about these lessons, nor do you need a daughter or sister. You just have to know a girl or a young woman and care about her future.

what girls need

Introduction

Challenges and Opportunities Awaiting Our Girls

As usual, I was running late for lunch. I quietly slipped into the packed dining room and slid into one of the last open chairs, my too-large handbag landing with a muffled thud on the faded rug beneath my feet. I pushed aside the bread and butter plate, whispered my Diet Coke order to a nearby waitress, and scanned the group gathered around the long tables to see whom I recognized.

It was my fourth of these lunch meetings with the Heads Club, an exclusive group of men and women who serve as senior administrators for the area's leading private schools. As equivalents of the CEOs of our schools, we met once a month to share updates, coordinate programmes, discuss policies that impact all our students, and talk about the challenges of leading a community of children, teachers, and parents wrestling with the social, political, financial, and other pressures of life in the twenty-first century. The room was filled with educators from schools in and around Philadelphia, New Jersey, and Delaware, including Catholic and Quaker schools, a number of co-educational schools, and a handful of all-boys and all-girls schools, plus a prestigious inner-city charter (grammar) school.

At this particular meeting, there were about twenty-five of us present, all community leaders at the pinnacle of careers in education. If you had been in the room with me, you would have watched twenty-five suit jackets tossed aside as we adjusted to the stuffy room, overheated by an ageing radiator hard at work on a cold winter day. You'd have heard twenty-five coffee cups clinking as we made room around the table for dessert. You'd also have noticed that there were twenty-three men present and only two women—a colleague seated on the opposite side of the crowded table, sipping her green tea, and me.

The day's lunchtime discussion wound through a handful of institutional concerns we all faced at our schools, including security on campus and students' mental health. Then, abruptly, a fellow head cleared his throat to get everyone's attention and take the conversation in a different direction.

"I want to talk about poaching," Kevin began. The annoyed look on his face suggested he'd been waiting throughout lunch to raise the issue. "Not just poaching one another's faculty but staff, too."

A murmur rippled through the group. Pilfering teachers was a sensitive subject, and a perennial discussion topic each year as top faculty became hot commodities. The end result was always a "gentleman's agreement" among Heads Club members,

Introduction

in which we all agreed not to actively steal teachers from one another.

"Of course, Kevin," responded Paul, a long-standing head of school who often served as the group's mediator when concerns arose. "It sounds like a good opportunity to revisit the understanding we all have about hiring each other's—"

Kevin interrupted before the sentence was complete. "That deal sounded great," Kevin said. "Until one of you stole someone from my admissions office."

A few folks shifted uncomfortably in their chairs. These meetings were usually collegial, rarely ever tense. The undercurrent of anger Kevin stirred up was surprising and awkward for us all.

"One of my admissions directors is now working for you, right, Laura?" Kevin said, nodding to the woman seated across from me at the table.

Laura looked startled. She put down her tea and scanned the room from end to end, clearly confused. "I have no idea what you're talking about," she said.

"Perhaps the gentleman's agreement doesn't apply, eh?" Kevin suggested with a smirk.

Suddenly the pieces of the puzzle began slotting together in my mind. I pictured the CV of a new member of my admissions team whom we'd hired a few weeks prior. I realized, belatedly, that she had previously worked for Kevin's school.

Kevin's disdain was focused on the wrong person. The wrong *woman*. His aggression was misdirected at Laura. His public put-down was meant for me.

For Women Everywhere, Challenges Remain

I was only mildly surprised by what unfolded at lunch that winter day. For years, I'd seen similar scenes play out everywhere I'd worked—in the West Wing of the White House, around conference tables at prestigious universities, in the briefing room aboard a Navy aircraft carrier. Verbal sparring was customary in almost all of these professional settings, as was the expectation that a woman wouldn't respond to such provocation by advocating for herself effectively. This wasn't the first time I'd seen a man take an aggressive public stance with a female colleague and assume he'd win simply by speaking first, by speaking loudly, or by speaking more confidently. I'd grown so used to "boys being boys" that I was more surprised when these dynamics *weren't* at play than when they were a force in the room.

When I started working in education, I imagined things would be different—not least because schools are places where women outnumber men. Approximately 77 per cent of teachers are women, a gender imbalance that has been steadily increasing over the past few decades as more women pursue careers as educators. But as it turns out, most of the senior officials and administrators at schools are male. Two-thirds of senior school heads, three-quarters of school district superintendents, and approximately two-thirds of private school heads are men. In fact, only recently did private schools move away from the gendered title "headmaster" and start using the neutral term "head

Introduction

of school". When it comes to the gender of those leading schools in comparison to those teaching in the classroom, the stereotypical imbalance remains firmly in place.

This pattern is likewise the case in almost any industry you pick—from higher education and academia to politics, business, the tech sector, and more. Gender disparities are entrenched, no matter where you look. This is still the reality awaiting our girls.

One recent study polled over 2,000 academics from two dozen universities to demonstrate that if a woman and a man have identical credentials—and a similar number of children and familial responsibilities—the man will have a more senior position and will have advanced further in his career than the woman. In other words, "being a woman has a negative association with academic rank". This scenario plays out in politics, too. Despite the record number of women running for and winning elections in the past few years, men still vastly outnumber women in elected political positions. In the United States, women hold just under a quarter of the seats in Congress despite making up greater than 50 per cent of the population. On the global stage, few countries come anywhere close to having gender parity in their government. The corporate world is no different. Women lead approximately 5 per cent of Fortune 500 companies and are similarly under-represented at all the senior levels of major businesses. Alarmingly, the gender gap has widened in the popular field of computer science. Women now earn only 18 per cent of the bachelor's degrees in computer science in the United States and make up less than 20 per cent of the workforce in related fields. Similar examples can be found in nearly any industry you choose.

What Girls Need

But it's not just numbers and demographics that shape the landscape our girls will have to navigate. Other gender disparities are still so firmly entrenched in modern society that they will no doubt be part of every young woman's life when she gets older. For example, while attempts to address pay inequities during the 1980s and 1990s helped narrow the gap in wages between women and men in America by over 16 per cent, progress in further closing this gap has stalled as of late: the gender earnings ratio—the most oft-cited way to compare women's average salary to men's—has closed by only 4.2 per cent since 2001. At the slowed rate of change, the date when women might reach pay equity with men has increasingly become more distant, moving from 2059 to 2119. Even in Denmark, which has long had established systems for promoting pay parity between men and women, efforts stalled.

Then there's the ever-present "motherhood penalty"—a catchy term for what happens when a woman gets pregnant and finds prize projects going to a colleague, worries that she will lose clients during maternity leave, or senses that a supervisor doubts her commitment to career advancement post-kids. In some instances, the mere idea that you might one day have children is enough to sideline women in a competitive workplace, meaning that the motherhood penalty can even impede the career progress of women who aren't planning to have kids.

Other subtle (and sometimes not-so-subtle) forms of gender bias are likewise still widespread, including biased promotion systems, sexual harassment, and more. Many women and men overlook these slights on a daily basis. But it's hard to ignore recent news that a prestigious law firm promoted a dozen people

Introduction

to the coveted role of partner—and all but one was a man; that a leading accounting firm is training its female employees on how to act nice around men, including how to avoid their tendency to "ramble and miss the point" in meetings; or that a female receptionist was sent home from the office because she was wearing ballet flats rather than the heels her employer had deemed mandatory for women. I know colleges work to attract my students and their female friends to areas where women are under-represented. I watch as corporate executives talk about building a better conduit into their industry for women and minorities. I hear from companies asking for advice on how to build better systems to support female employees. Yet gender-based norms remain in place.

So I wasn't surprised to hear from Brianna, a final-year student at my school, a few weeks after I spoke with her class about gender bias in the workplace. She'd just finished an after-school activity in which she was teaming with a group of boys on a community project. With our classroom discussion in mind, she suddenly realized that her teenage friends were replicating the gender norms that research shows are common barriers for adult women in the wider world. During a long afternoon working on the project, Brianna noticed that the boys were using breaks to "network" with kids they didn't know and with adult advisors in the room, while the girls stuck to their friend groups. She was also astonished to recognize when, after she had shared her opinion on a controversial topic, "one of our male friends behind us popped into the circle and essentially repeats exactly what I just said." It was her first exposure to that "funny, but not really" sensation so many adult women have when they're experiencing mansplaining. Brianna concluded that even though she and her friends weren't yet in the working world, they were all still acting out the gendered behaviours typical of adults.

For the first time, she consciously noticed the habits—and the pitfalls—that working women have been dealing with for years. It didn't matter that the girls and boys were just fifteen and sixteen years old, hadn't yet had their first real job, and considered themselves part of a generation free of many norms that held back their parents. As it turns out, some things hadn't changed at all.

It's therefore disappointing but not shocking to read the Bill & Melinda Gates Foundation's latest report examining inequity around the globe and to see their conclusion that "no matter where you are born, your life will be harder if you are born a girl." Brianna's personal experience came right on schedule: according to the research, the trajectory of girls' and boys' futures starts to diverge in adolescence.

That's why we, as parents and teachers, must prepare children from an early age to recognize, refute, and push back against the gender biases and discrimination that are still a daily reality for women around the world. Advocating for systemic change— including efforts to overhaul workplace standards, modify laws and regulations, introduce new support structures for victims of sexual harassment, and celebrate gains made by individuals or small groups—is only a small part of the solution. We also need to be honest about the particular gender-specific challenges that our girls will face when they're older—especially since systematic changes won't have maximum effect for a generation or even two—and work to better prepare our young women to tackle these realities. We need to ensure they have the critical skills they need to succeed despite the entrenched norms.

This is where little things matter a lot, and where the lessons of *What Girls Need* can make a lasting difference for years to come.

For Kids Everywhere, New Opportunities on the Horizon

When Kara, a cheerful middle school student with long brown hair and an easy smile, steps to the podium, she's gripping her typed notes tightly with both hands. She is about to speak in front of the entire school, over seven hundred people including her classmates, favourite teachers, and a handful of parents. This is a daunting task for most of us, but especially for a thirteen-year-old during her first week of school. Kara steals a glance at a senior student to her right for reassurance and, with a deep breath and an eye on the papers now crumpled in front of her, launches into her remarks.

"To me, the future means the time that I have not planned for yet," she begins, the words spilling out rapidly because of her excitement and nervous energy. "I have planned that I will be in school through college, but after that it seems to be open... What will I do when that time comes?

What Girls Need

"A majority of the jobs that we Baldwin girls will have are not yet invented," Kara explains, then courageously admits: "That has always fascinated me, and to be honest, scared me a little."

Kara is not alone in this feeling. When she and her friends think about the future, what worries them is the unknown nature of what's to come, the fact that things are impossible to predict. Whether they are wondering what will happen to their favourite social media influencer or imagining what life will look like when they're older, there are no clear answers. The most reliable thing we know about the future is that it's largely unknown.

But predicting the future is also what every parent and educator regularly tries to do. We typically don't think about our work as mothers, fathers, teachers, and coaches in that way, not least because it makes the daily details of raising kids seem that much more overwhelming. Nevertheless, when we are looking for advice concerning the girls we love—what class she should take next, whether she should try a new sport, or how she should navigate a tough moment with friends—we are also searching for answers to broader, bigger questions. When should we lend support or clear the path of hurdles, so that we nurture and protect but still build confidence and resilience? How will any single decision impact our daughters for years to come? In other words, what can we do to prepare our girls for the world that awaits them when they're older?

This is where a little fortune-telling can be helpful. While we can't say with certainty what the workplace and world of tomorrow will look like or how the ever-changing job market will

Introduction

unfold, a close look at trends already under way can give us a glimpse into the decades ahead. And when the studies of the future work are paired with an understanding of girls' social, emotional, and intellectual development, we discover guideposts for what lessons today's school-aged kids need most and how to tailor what we do—and how we do it—with girls in mind.

Consider, for example, the effect of rapid technological change over the past decade and how it influences the types of jobs and skills our children will need as adults. Technological innovation, especially artificial intelligence and big-data analytics, has rapidly accelerated the pace of transformation in the twenty-first century. What's more, we also have to consider other mega-trends, like globalization, urbanization, and demographic shifts in developed and undeveloped countries. The next few decades are expected to see major economic and social changes that influence how we define "work"—both what jobs we do and how we do them—in years to come. According to former treasury secretary, Harvard University president, and renowned economist Lawrence Summers, this changing nature of work will be "the defining economic feature of our era." The impact of technological innovation on the workforce is particularly important for our youngest students, whose lives will bridge the twenty-first and twenty-second centuries; it will no doubt redefine what jobs are available, what the workplace looks like when today's girls are adults, and what skills will be required to be successful in the next century.

For example, while the fear that robots will dominate every profession is overstated, automation and artificial intelligence will no doubt fundamentally alter how a lot of jobs are performed. The influence of the Internet of Things and digitization, a fancy term for what happens when everyday things—like a car part, an article of clothing, or even a piece of food—are transformed into bits and bytes for production by a 3-D printer, also means that our girls will have work we can't even imagine right now. In fact, many of the jobs today's young professionals are most eager to pursue—from digital art curator to social media analyst—directly reflect the influence of these innovations and are jobs that didn't even exist five years ago. As thirteen-year-old Kara pointed out, 65 per cent of kids now entering primary school will one day work in a job that hasn't yet been created. And the World Economic Forum recently estimated that 133 million new jobs may be created as a result of technological change.

Globalization and the increased interconnectedness that technology allows will also impact not just *what* today's kids do when they're adults but also *how* they do it. More and more, navigating the future workforce and the wider world will require that our girls be comfortable interacting with different cultures and people and be able to work with others regardless of background. Yes, they need the solid literacy, numeracy, and related skills one expects from a traditional school. But they must also successfully communicate, collaborate, and self-organize while navigating complex cultural dynamics and differences.

What does all of this mean for today's kids—or more specifically, for our girls? Are there things we need to do to prepare them for what is to come? How can we position them to thrive as this new future unfolds?

To effectively embrace the opportunities that will come during the decades ahead, our kids need a new set of twenty-first-century skills. Today's students must be taught to be adaptive learners skilled at abstract reasoning and flexible thinking in context, prepared for a world requiring human creativity, coordination, and decision-making that leverages information provided by artificial intelligence. They need the ability to analyze information, deal with uncertainty, and tackle challenges in multidisciplinary ways, no matter what job they pursue—or invent—when they're older. And they need to be flexible, collaborative problem-solvers skilled at drawing connections across disciplines, communicating across boundaries, and adapting well in teams. Research shows our girls naturally do all of these things quite well, particularly if we nurture their innate talents from an early age.

The ability to identify, the support to nurture, and the wherewithal to use these important twenty-first-century skills is what our girls need for a still-being-defined future.

For the moment, let's turn our attention back to the Heads Club lunch that dry winter day. In response to Kevin's public accusation, Laura, my fellow female head, guardedly defended herself against the claim that she'd "poached" another school's staff member. Other heads of school around the table whispered to one another, both curious about and disconcerted by the tension and conflict. Our overly sweet desserts sat uneaten as we waited for the soap opera's closing scene.

Which is when I gingerly raised my hand, motioning to Kevin at the other end of the table. "I'm not completely sure," I started, admittedly uncertain about both the details of this hiring dispute and my decision to jump into the middle of the debate, "but I'm pretty sure you mean *me*, Kevin."

The additional qualifier "the *other* woman in the room" went unspoken. Everyone in the room quickly sensed what happened. Kevin had confused the two women at the lunch meeting—the only two women in a room full of school leaders.

"I think my school hired one of your admissions directors recently," I said bluntly. "I'm sure someone called members of your team for reference checks."

I paused, waiting to see if my memory of the events would get traction with Kevin, then continued, "Apologies if there was any confusion along the way, and that I never called to discuss it directly with you." According to the unwritten rules, an open discussion between heads was protocol in these hiring situations.

I scanned the room, trying to read my colleagues' expressions. I didn't want to lose their support or trust, and wasn't sure how my directness would be received.

A few seconds passed. Then I saw some restrained shrugs and heard the sound of forks diving into slices of warm pecan pie. My admission broke the tension, and the description of my team's standard process made sense. Plus, to my relief, my bluntness did not exacerbate an already tense situation but instead was brushed aside like the bread crumbs still scattered around the lunch table.

Kevin squinted and his eyes registered confusion, but he recovered quickly. He'd realized his mistake. "Yes, yes," he agreed, "it was your school. That's right. You hired one of our enrollment officers and we never got a call."

Within seconds, Kevin's enthusiasm for verbal sparring had subsided. It hadn't helped that he couldn't even remember which head of school—that is to say, which woman—he had an issue with. Or that his challenger had so readily come forward to take ownership of the miscommunication and advocate for herself.

In a flash, I recalled how the men I'd served with in the Navy resolved similar semi-public skirmishes in our squadron ready room. "Seems like I owe you a bottle of wine," I said to Kevin. "Let me know what you like."

He shrugged and pulled his dessert dish closer. The moment had passed. There was no need to continue jousting.

Twenty minutes later, when everyone had devoured their pecan pie and was loitering to chat, I pulled Kevin aside. "Kevin, apologies once again if we missed a step in our screening process. Or if you were unaware of our plans to hire a member of your staff," I began. "But in the future, if you have an issue, just call. There's no need to make it a public argument. Always happy to talk things over."

I never heard what wine he liked, though Kevin did later email to apologize for, in his own words, "calling me out". The lesson learned from my naval aviation days had worked; ironically, calling Kevin out for calling me out helped quickly resolve things. Nevertheless, I now wear a hard-to-miss pin with my school's emblem on my blazer as a way to clearly distinguish me from the other brunette in the room.

What Girls Need

With all the modern world asks us to juggle, the pressing question for parents and educators becomes what can we do on a daily basis to prepare today's young girls to make the most of what awaits them as adults. How can we ensure our kids are empowered to tackle any challenge they face and embrace every opportunity that comes their way? What little things matter most? And how can we tailor our approach to best serve our daughters?

This is where a lot of books introduce concepts like confidence, resilience, and bravery—all important traits for our girls to develop, even though most of us would likely admit we still struggle to model these ideal attributes many years into adulthood. They are lofty goals to set for any school-aged kid. So what if, rather than focusing on these broader traits, we take a closer look at the daily business of "adulting" to see how practical aspects of these qualities reveal themselves and help define what our girls will need in the real world. In other words, instead of confining ourselves to the definition of terms, let's explore key skills that women need to thrive in and out of the workplace, now and for decades to come.

To do so, I'll use social science research alongside input from

Introduction

girls, parents, and teachers to investigate the major roadblocks and opportunities that young women must be ready to overcome and embrace when they're older. Each chapter also shares my personal stories and anecdotes from female colleagues making waves from Wall Street to Silicon Valley, from the E Ring of the Pentagon to senior levels of Hollywood, to demonstrate which lessons from childhood were most critical as we navigated the working world and beyond. I also discuss the lessons we missed along the way. By exploring what our girls need in this way, we discover how quantifiable, teachable skills nurtured early on provide our girls with the solid foundation essential for success and satisfaction later in life.

In the first three chapters, I'll address some of the major challenges that still hold many women back—hurdles that our girls can be prepared to leap over, with a little bit of early coaching. Chapter 1 focuses on why we must help girls grow comfortable with speaking their mind and ensure that they learn to effectively use their voice from a young age. I'll explore how to help school-aged girls become effective self-advocates, a vital aspect of growing into successful adult women—not just as a tool to combat sexual harassment and discrimination, but because the future world of work will require this skill of both women and men even more than it does today. Chapter 2 builds on these ideas to describe how to teach girls the important art and science of asking. So they can speak up for themselves and are prepared to persuade, negotiate, and get what they need as adults, in all aspects of life. Chapter 3 describes why it's likewise critical for our daughters to develop a healthy competitive spirit, illustrating how this is often a challenge for girls and young women. As is true with all the chapters, it shares practical advice for small steps that can help build your daughter's skill set in this area.

The next three chapters focus on future changes that await our children, identifying transformations likely to impact the next generation and exploring how girls' natural talents can be their competitive advantage in this new landscape. Chapter 4 outlines one of the most critical skills for the twenty-first-century working world: the ability to collaboratively solve complex problems. It's a skill that comes naturally to young girls and should be fostered from an early age, to give young women a future advantage no matter what career they pursue. Chapter 5 focuses on empathy, another essential skill for the next generation. It explores how to help your daughter tap into her natural empathic potential, so her innate ability to understand another's point of view becomes a powerful tool that she can leverage in adulthood, personally and professionally. To complete our discussion of what our girls need most for their still-unfolding future, Chapter 6 looks at adaptability. This chapter describes tailored, girl-centric ways to nurture your daughter's willingness to take risks, embrace change, and face uncertainty, while building her resilience and love of learning—giving her the adaptive expertise that will be so critical to success in the decades to come.

As we dive into this discussion, here are a few caveats to consider. First, while this book focuses specifically on girls, any parent will realize that many of the concepts are equally applicable to boys. Young men also need to be good at speaking up and advocating for themselves, negotiating and networking,

Introduction

collaborative problem-solving, and more. And those lessons should likewise start from a young age. Of course!

That said, the focus on girls here is critical. While there are some girls (and women) who've already mastered what we'll discuss, research and personal experience suggest that, by and large, these are areas in which women lag behind their male peers. What's more, society has historically nurtured many of these skills in boys and ensured that they become areas where men generally have a competitive advantage. While individual childhood experiences and personality differences make everyone's strengths and weaknesses unique, there is no doubt that exposing girls to tailored lessons early on would help bridge remaining gender gaps.

Also keep in mind that, while some traits we'll discuss have historically been called "masculine", I am not arguing that women need to behave like men to succeed. Or that women need to change their personalities or adjust their definition of success to conform to societal norms. Indeed, no judgement is made about those who consciously decide not to self-advocate, negotiate, compete, or otherwise use the tools described in this book. But for many women, me included, not using these skills isn't a choice we deliberately make but an unintended consequence of the situations we find ourselves in. Because we didn't learn the lessons of this book early on, we find it harder to speak up, to ask for what we need, and to compete for what we want when we're older. *What Girls Need* aims to ensure that all girls have every critical life skill at their disposal when they become adults, faced with new challenges or exciting opportunities.

What Girls Need

In fact, I chose to concentrate on these skills and traits because research shows they are beneficial to both men and women, personally and professionally—even as many are currently areas where men typically dominate. But what if self-advocacy, negotiating, competing, problem-solving, and more were considered gender-neutral traits? What if we nurture these talents in girls early on so that they organically develop a personal approach to using these skills, empowering them to define success as an adult on their own terms? That is the goal of this book, with each chapter providing practical age-specific advice for introducing these ideas to your girls.

Finally, a note about how this approach fits into the broader landscape of literature on girls and women—particularly debates about how to address sexual harassment, the gender pay gap, women's under-representation in certain sectors, and family leave. The chapters ahead focus on how every girl can be better prepared for the realities of the future working world. But I do not discount the importance of continued systemic change, including ongoing efforts to adapt institutions and policies that remain barriers to entry for women and girls or for minority groups. Those efforts must continue and should be supported by every anxious parent, doting grandparent, and attentive teacher while we also do our best to prepare today's girls for the likely realities of adulthood.

Even with these caveats in mind, we must candidly discuss— and debate!—how to effectively prepare our girls. We need to consider areas in which many adult women lag behind men and decide how we can best guide our girls when they're young,

Introduction

so they can thrive in situations where we ourselves may have stumbled.

So as you turn the pages in the chapters ahead, also think about each skill in the context of your own moments of failure—those big or little belly flops of life, when you realized in retrospect that you'd been ill prepared. As each chapter unfolds, ask yourself what part of your own story fits best. And don't hesitate to share those personal lessons with your daughter, too. Your experience and humility might give her a leg up when she's in similar situations. It's another step towards helping every girl get what she needs to succeed.

Help Her Find Her Voice

J ocelyn's email starts with the formal opening and directness of someone years her senior. "Good Evening, Dr Barnes. I am not sure if you remember me, but my name is Jocelyn and I am a first-year in senior school."

The email continues, briefly mentioning her connection to the college that Dr Barnes oversees before quickly turning to her reason for writing. "I would like to report an incident that happened on your campus last night around 8:15 p.m."

Jocelyn then describes being sexually harassed one summer evening while walking with her friend Kate through a neighbourhood college campus. In her letter to the college president, she succinctly depicts the art-room entrance where two men were loitering. She details what the men were wearing, describing the employees' uniforms down to the official school emblem on their collared shirts. And how the men first greeted her and Kate in a friendly tone, as they all exchanged pleasant hellos in passing. Then she describes the sexual harassment that quickly followed.

"As we walked away, they began catcalling us by saying 'Damn, you girls are pretty. Come back here,' and whistling. They made repulsive comments," she continues, alluding to the shouts that trailed behind the girls as they continued on through the campus—observations about Kate's body, lewd comments about the casual summer dress Jocelyn was wearing, and descriptions of indecent things they wanted to do to the girls behind closed doors.

"We feared for our safety," Jocelyn says, noting how the two friends sprinted to the protection of her mum's idling car, hoping they could outrun the shouts dogging them through campus.

Jocelyn is sixteen years old. Kate is learning to drive but still needs to practise parallel parking. They both love singing and are tied to their cell phones. Their parents think they spend too much time on social media, though Kate speaks with pride of her summer job as a lifeguard and Jocelyn is excited to have been chosen as head of the school's community service group. Now these two confident and curious girls were running for the family car, shaking with fear.

Despite how much they just wanted to relish the feeling of being safely in the car, with Jocelyn's mum there to support and protect them, Jocelyn and Kate instead sat there drafting a note to the long-standing college president, a middle-aged man whom they knew from a distance and saw at community events. They asked that the two men be held accountable for their actions. They wanted to know "what your school's policy is on sexual harassment by an employee." The teenagers also wondered "if you have any training in place . . . on sexual harassment," noting without a hint of irony that "if you do, I think they need a refresher."

Kate and Jocelyn still had curfews and couldn't technically see an R-rated movie by themselves. Their parents were still hesitant to let them date. But these teenage girls already knew how to self-advocate effectively.

When I first heard this story, in an informal incident report confidentially shared by administrators at the college where my students had been harassed, I was shocked, appalled, and concerned for the girls' well-being. A few minutes later, after I skimmed Jocelyn's email, which had been forwarded along with a sincere and apologetic cover letter, I was incredibly proud of how these teenagers responded.

Would I have crafted such a clearly written, maturely argued note of formal protest at their age, especially in the wake of this sort of traumatic and confusing encounter? Doubtful. Would most young women? Not according to the research, which suggests that only 20 per cent of female college students take steps to file a report after being sexually assaulted. Would most adult women? That's unlikely, too. Three out of four people who experience harassment at work never even mention it to a supervisor or manager, and making an official complaint is by far the least common response.

This reality becomes even more troubling when we consider how a girl's decision to speak out or remain silent—and for a woman to self-advocate or not—impacts her daily life, personally and professionally. It's not just about sexual harassment or sexual assault, even while those are clear areas of concern. It's also about how women are taught to voice their opinions, ideas, and needs at work, at home, or at a bar. And how we can more effectively teach this critical but often overlooked skill, from an early age.

H aving spotted the placard with my name on it at one end of the long wooden conference table, I settled into a stiff upholstered chair and looked around the Roosevelt Room. After many weekends giving informal tours of the West Wing to family and friends, I knew the details behind each piece of historic memorabilia in this White House meeting room, just next to the Oval Office.

From my spot at the end of the table, I had a clear view of a famous portrait of Teddy Roosevelt hanging above the fireplace, depicting the president aloft a horse, in his Rough Rider garb. Roosevelt's 1906 Nobel Peace Prize gleamed in one corner, across from a wall of flags representing each military service and every battle fought by U.S. soldiers, sailors, and marines. I also knew that the peephole in the door at the room's other corner was actually a reverse looking glass, through which you could watch people coming and going from the Oval Office.

My eyes settled on the empty seat a few feet away, five spots to my right, at the centre of the gleaming rectangular conference table. Where there was no placard. Where no placard was needed. There was no chance anyone would mistakenly sit there, and President Obama knew which seat was his.

A discreet buzz filled the room while we waited for the president to arrive, as colleagues around the table quietly chatted with whoever was seated to their left or right. The fourteen friends and co-workers joining me that day, all White House Fellows, were an accomplished bunch and one of the most diverse groups I'd seen in my career. Since we'd been selected with both our professional experience and personal backgrounds in mind, the group included battle-hardened soldiers, financial wizards, emergency room doctors, and others—plus there were almost as many women as men, and a third were minorities. I was proud not only to have made the cut but also to know that the pool of those considered for the job was talented, diverse, and committed to making the future better for the next generation. We'd all been eagerly awaiting our informal meeting with the leader of the free world.

A few minutes after the hour, President Obama walked into the room, followed shortly by an assistant carrying a dainty ceramic teacup emblazoned with the presidential seal. We stood to greet him, and I was struck by the fact that his genuine smile didn't mask the fatigue in his eyes. Just in that week alone, there had been a foiled terrorist attack in Texas for which the Islamic State was taking credit. Four earthquakes had struck the San Francisco area, while a flurry of tornadoes had ravaged the Midwest. Oil prices hit a low point, raising concerns for the economy and U.S. relations with the Middle East. And news would soon come out that Vice President Biden's son Beau had lost his battle with brain cancer. A typical Thursday for the president of the United States, and the bags under his eyes reflected the fact that there was a lot on his mind.

Over the next hour, the group peppered President Obama with questions as he sat sipping hot tea, subtly sucking on a cough drop to ward off an apparent cold. The conversation ranged from his strategies for making tough decisions and his approach to building teams to issues like climate change, weapons of mass destruction, and income inequality. He spoke candidly about why regular dinners with his wife and kids were so personally and professionally important, and shared what worried him for the country's future.

I had worked for years to earn a seat at the proverbial table—and had made it to one of the most powerful tables in the world, a few feet from the president of the United States. But as colleagues around the table chimed in regularly, sometimes commenting about my areas of national security expertise, I stayed silent.

During one of the most exciting opportunities of my career thus far, I didn't say a word.

"If You're Not Assertive, You Don't Get Very Far"

No doubt all women can remember a moment when we didn't speak up. When we didn't voice our opinion or share our ideas, especially in a group or at work. Or when we weren't effectively assertive in a difficult personal or professional situation. The question, of course, is whether that moment was pivotal to your success. Does it really matter? Did it make a difference? Is the ability to gather your thoughts, voice your opinion, and assert yourself a skill that our girls definitively need to thrive later in life?

The answer, of course, is that owning your voice is a personal superpower that every girl needs to succeed. The ability to turn inward confidence into action by speaking out is one of the most crucial life skills your daughter will rely on, as a young adult and for years to come. This is true not just in moments of crisis like the sexual harassment that Jocelyn and Kate experienced, but while she is reckoning with the everyday realities of work and life as a woman.

Nurturing your girl's ability to speak up effectively for herself is critical to encouraging her independence, both intellectually and emotionally. Feeling confident that she can harness her voice helps her calmly and respectfully navigate the ups and downs of school, manage relationships with friends and teachers, and respond to real-world challenges in the moment. As she gets older, self-advocacy will also be critical in any team she joins, in any job she pursues—particularly in a world where working in groups will increasingly become the norm. Decades of sociological and psychological research also underscore that a person's ability to speak up and capably assert herself in a group setting is critical to gaining and maintaining influence and to eliciting support from others. Indeed, some studies suggest that the amount you verbally participate in group discussions may be the largest factor in how much influence you have.

For real-world examples of this, consider role models like Colonel Abigail Linnington, a career army officer who rose through the military's ranks—beginning her career as a helicopter pilot in the demilitarized zone between North and South Korea, and ultimately becoming a trusted advisor to the chairman of the Joint Chiefs of Staff, the most senior officer in the U.S. military forces. When I was struggling to navigate a difficult career transition and turned to her for advice, she shared that the key to her success was her willingness to speak up.

"Being assertive is as important as anything else. Perhaps more important," she noted, pausing to mentally reflect on her professional path. "Especially the higher up you go. People need to see you speak up, in order to gain confidence in you. That's when soldiers follow you. When they believe in your leadership.

"If you weren't assertive, you didn't get very far."

I t's hard for many women, me included, to effectively and appropriately assert themselves in mixed-gender environments, whether at work or at home. Even today, there are countless examples from every sector imaginable of women and girls who don't have an influential voice in whatever conversation is unfolding around them. We can all no doubt picture the situations described in scientific studies that show female college students are less likely than their male peers to ask or answer a question in class, that women receive less credit than men for their contributions to group projects at work, and that girls are judged as less competent and less employable than boys because of speech patterns common to both genders. And that in many cases, when women do try to speak up, they are dismissed. Ignored. Even shushed.

These sorts of enduring inequities, which women are so used to facing, were one reason why a particular lunchtime workshop during the weeklong SXSW (South by Southwest) Conference in Austin in 2015 attracted a few thousand spectators. The moderated discussion was about a hot topic—innovation in the digital era—and featured three of the top names in the tech industry: Megan J. Smith, chief technology officer of the United States; Eric Schmidt, executive chairman of Google; and Walter Isaacson, president and CEO of the Aspen Institute and author of a well-known biography of Steve Jobs, among other bestsellers.

As the three speakers settled into plush leather seats onstage at the Austin Conference Center, Megan Smith naturally stood out. Her emerald-green blouse was the sole splash of colour on the dais. She was also the only woman on the panel, and one of the few women scheduled as a headline tech speaker at that year's SXSW. Not unusual, of course, for the industry or conferences like these more generally. Men make up approximately 70 per cent of all panel speakers at professional conferences, and the number hovers around 80 per cent when the subject under discussion is technology. All-male panels, jokingly called "manels" by some, are still so common that scientists, foreign policy experts, journalists, and more have started grassroots movements to address the imbalance in their industries even as social media sites make light of the situation.

During this particular hour-long session, the esteemed panel talked about the impact of innovation on business, government and popular culture, artificial intelligence, immigration, broadband access, and more. They also spent a lot of time fielding questions about diversity and inclusion: how to recruit, support, and fund more women and people of colour, and how to accelerate these sorts of human capital innovations in tech and other industries.

But as the discussion unfolded, what was most noticeable was how much the two men onstage interrupted the lone woman on their panel—even during questions directed to her specifically, as when Smith was talking about family leave and Schmidt interrupted to chime in. At one point, the Google chairman directed Megan on what questions she should answer, and offered to respond to a query from the audience on her behalf. She took the likely unconscious but nonetheless obvious sexism in stride, even smiling and joking at one point when she was blatantly cut off, but it was awkward for everyone listening.

Eventually the audience grew tired of watching the most senior government official overseeing technology policy for the entire country being shushed by her male colleagues. So when the microphone was passed to an audience member for a question, Judith Williams, Google's diversity programme manager, stepped to the front of the conference centre hall to ask about unconscious bias. And to point out what was obvious to everyone watching.

"Research tells us that women are interrupted a lot more than men," Williams began as Isaacson grinned sheepishly and Schmidt squirmed a bit in his chair, "and I wonder if you are aware that you have interrupted Megan many more times than you have interrupted each other."

The crowd cheered and applauded. Neither of the male panelists responded. They'd suddenly lost their voices.

▌ What Does the Research Show?

To understand how to help girls learn to become effective self-advocates, we need to consider why it remains so difficult for many women to speak up. And why when they do, what women say is not received as well and often fails to have as much influence as they'd hoped. What conscious or unconscious biases create barriers for our girls as they try to raise their voice? What social, cultural, or other expectations impact women's—and men's—ability to be heard, particularly in mixed-gender environments?

For decades, social scientists have tried to solve this long-standing cultural puzzle by studying how conversations unfold between women and men, at home and at work, and what factors most influence the apparent gender-based inequities that impact a person's ability to self-advocate. Since the 1970s, linguists, psychologists, and other social scientists have focused on how and when we talk, how women and men perceive one another's speech, and how gender impacts the influence of our words. The aim in part was to figure out why there's been a long-held perception that women speak more than men—even when that idea is proven false in numerous contexts, and even when men more often hold the power in mixed-gender conversations. How should we explain the fact that we're raised to believe that girls are (too) talkative when in fact at work and in class, in meetings and formal public or semi-public contexts, women speak less, are often silenced or interrupted, and don't effectively self-advocate as a result?

Fundamental to this work was a socio-linguistic study conducted in 1975 by two sociology professors from the University of California who wanted to understand whether women and men speak differently—and if so, why. Don Zimmerman and Candace West had long been interested in language and gender, so they decided to explore the topic further by recording thirty-one conversations in coffee shops, pharmacies, and other public places around a college town where people typically gather for routine chitchat. By and large, the speakers were white and in their twenties to early thirties—with two-thirds of the groups being same-sex pairings (i.e. two men or two women speaking) while eleven were female–male pairs. Conversation ranged from discussions about ordinary life to quarrels between lovers and even to casual pleasantries people exchanged during their first meeting. Despite the seeming randomness in both the types of pairs and the conversations that were recorded, one thing held steady: in the mixed-sex pairs, men interrupted much more than women, on the order of forty-six to two.

While gender is just one factor that influences people's

conversational styles and impacts how and when they speak up, researchers built on the work of Zimmerman and West to prove that gender bias has an outsized impact on how women are heard in any setting they find themselves in, from the conference table at the office to the dinner table at home. In the words of Deborah Tannen, a professor of linguistics at Georgetown University who has spent decades studying interpersonal communication styles, the "different socialization patterns of boys and girls makes meetings a very different environment for men and women." She found, in short, that boys are conditioned from a young age to feel comfortable speaking up in groups—and are thus given the natural advantage as adults, in meetings and similar professional settings.

Time and again, other social scientists have backed these findings in laboratories and the real world. The result is a disheartening picture of how conversations and power asymmetries play out in the working world—whether you're in law or academia, tech or medicine, or a number of other industries. As demonstrated by academic research, countless personal stories, and news reports, too, when women are in male-dominated arenas, they are more often "interrupted, talked over, shut down, or penalized for speaking out." Even in the Supreme Court, female justices are at a disadvantage when it comes to speaking up to influence public discussions. During oral arguments, they are disproportionately interrupted by the male justices and even by male lawyers arguing before the court, despite the fact that procedural rules technically prohibit a lawyer from interrupting a justice. In 2015, for example, 65.9 per cent of all interruptions during Supreme Court proceedings were directed at Ruth Bader Ginsburg, Sonia Sotomayor, and Elena Kagan, the three female justices on the bench. Even the most senior and seasoned female judges in the country are silenced by male peers and subordinates. Given the important role that oral arguments play in deciding cases, this unfortunate gender-based norm can also hinder their ability to influence the outcome of a case.

In academia, a similar phenomenon is found in the number of opportunities that women are given to participate on prestigious panels—the university equivalent of important meetings in a boardroom, where rising stars have their ideas heard, build their reputations, and gather support from peers and seniors. A 2018 study by professors at Rice University showed that men gave over twice as many speeches at important academic conferences for a range of disciplines—from biology to political science and history—even after controlling for the gender of available speakers. Women didn't decline invitations to speak at these panels more often than men, nor did they find these colloquia less valuable than their male peers did. They simply weren't invited to speak.

Other real-world studies provide evidence that women speak less and are interrupted more than men—whether you look at the tech industry, where men are almost three times more likely to interrupt a woman than a man despite widespread gender disparity in Silicon Valley, the medical field, local school boards, or even in the online comment section of *The New York Times*. In the latter, an eight-month study of online remarks made to the newspaper's news articles showed that women represented just

28 per cent of participants. They were speaking up less, despite the protection and anonymity provided by the internet.

The disheartening truth is that even in the twenty-first century, women are often "seen but not heard"—and that reality is unfortunately normalized with kids from an early age. Consider one study of girls and boys playing together after school, where groups of two to four preschool children and early primary school students ranging from three and a half to six and a half years old were observed at play dates over an eight-week period. During ten plus hours of playtime, the girls and boys were monitored to see how often they interrupted one another and to track the gender of the playmate they interrupted. At first glance, the researcher—a mother of a "chatty four-year-old" who was accustomed to being constantly interrupted by her daughter—noted that groups with and without boys had about the same number of interruptions per hour. For both groups, a child interrupted his or her friend about once every minute and seventeen seconds.

But when this researcher dug further, to consider who was doing the interrupting and whose voice was being shut down in the process, she found that in co-educational playgroups, boys interrupted almost three times as often as girls did. More disconcerting, as the number of boys in the group increased, the girls grew quieter and quieter; for example, when a group of three boys was playing with one girl, the girl spoke up just twice while the boys interrupted each other fifty-three times in an hour. The corollary is also true. When there were no boys in the group, the girls spoke out—and interrupted—just as often as the boys did.

When boys are around, they dominate and girls withdraw

from whatever conversation is under way. Take the boys out of the picture and the girls' voices come out loud and strong. Just like the boys'. In other words, the dynamic that we see at the SXSW panel, in a doctor's office, at the Supreme Court, and in so many more working environments starts on the playground, when our daughters are barely four years old.

J ust a few hours after sending their email, Kate and Jocelyn received a reply from Dr Barnes, the college president. He asked the girls to return to campus to discuss the incident and the school's response, in person. Within a day, the two teenagers were sitting on a worn brown leather couch in his office, flanked by the president, the school's head of security, and the director of human resources.

"Thank you for immediately letting me know what happened," Dr Barnes began after his trademark opening banter, which he hoped would put the girls at ease. "You responded very maturely and completely appropriately, in a very uncomfortable situation. I am grateful that you provided us with the information we needed to hold these men responsible for their actions."

A short conversation followed where the security director explained that the entire incident had been recorded by a tucked-away security camera. He described how an investigation was formally under way, offering to take notes on any other information Jocelyn and Kate wished to share. When the girls admitted there wasn't much else to say, they were given the chance to watch the video of what happened. Both swiftly responded with

"Nah ... Thanks anyway." Having experienced the harassment first-hand, they felt no need to replay the whole exchange.

The director of human resources congratulated the girls for how they handled themselves. With a comforting, motherly smile, she also assured them that their confidentiality would be protected. Dr Barnes closed the short formal meeting with an energetic handshake, sharing that he planned to write both girls' families and commend them for their actions.

A few months later, when Jocelyn and Kate talk about the entire ordeal, they casually shrug it away.

"I've been through worse," shares Kate, describing an incident in which her fourteen-year-old friend was groped from behind on a Philadelphia pavement, as the two teenagers were walking to get ice cream one afternoon.

But when I ask the girls to consider *why* they responded the way they did to the sexual harassment that unfolded that summer night—and whether all their friends would have done the same—they quickly glance at each other for validation. Kate shrugs and shifts in her seat. Jocelyn tugs at the black scrunchie on her wrist.

"I didn't realize it was out of the ordinary to stand up for yourself in that way," admits Jocelyn. "But I can think of friends who wouldn't do the same..." Her voice trails off, as if she doesn't want to share friends' secrets.

My question hangs in the air between us. Why are some women—and some young girls—good at asserting themselves and some aren't? How can these girls already know how to authoritatively, respectfully, and effectively speak up, even in the face of aggressive harassment? Even when talking to a senior male executive about such an uncomfortable situation?

And how can we ensure that every girl—and every adult woman—learns critical life skills of self-advocacy, from an early age?

What's a Parent to Do?

Ultimately, every parent wants to help their daughter become her own most active and effective cheerleader. But it's a daunting task, particularly given the social, emotional, and societal hurdles that our girls face on a daily basis—many of which we've discussed in this chapter, even as countless other factors come into play depending on race and background, geography and community norms, who else is in the room, and more.

Fortunately, little things can have a sizable impact on how girls develop the skills and attitude that make the biggest difference here. Some of the most effective strategies for helping a girl develop her voice from a young age involve very small steps that parents, teachers, and other trusted adults can take to help every young woman practise the act of "speaking up" in an age-appropriate way that suits her personality. No, this doesn't mean that an introverted girl must become an extrovert or that your pre-teenage daughter should be allowed to talk back or confuse disrespect with self-advocacy. Rather, it's about finding natural ordinary moments when your girl might normally be quiet and turning these into opportunities to help her practise using her voice. Effective self-advocacy is a skill like any other. It requires practice.

What does this practice look like? For starters, consciously talk with your daughter about how she participates—or doesn't—in class or her favourite activity. This conversation isn't aimed at producing quantifiable results and it's not about pushing her to be more talkative just for the sake of talking. Instead, it's about demonstrating the importance of her vocally participating in whatever way suits her best. So starting when she's in primary school, consider what questions about her day will prompt her to understand the value of her voice. Rather than simply asking, "What did you do today?" or "How was science class?" perhaps you can draw out specifically what question she asked her teacher that day or whether she mentioned in science the funny-looking bug she found in the backyard over the weekend. The goal is to help our girls discover natural paths where their thoughts, opinions, and advocacy reveal themselves. By highlighting those moments and reflecting on them with her, you also reinforce the idea that your daughter's participation in and assertiveness at school are as important as the subjects she's learning.

Along the same lines, consider how you involve your daughter in what otherwise might feel like "adult" conversations at home. When a debate unfolds at the dinner table or in the car, about something on the news or even just about whether a movie you saw was worth the price of admission, consciously invite your daughter to participate. Encourage her from a young age to engage in the group's discussion—and to debate with you, too. At first it may feel scripted or stiff for you and embarrassing or awkward for your daughter, but it will leave a lasting impression with her about the value of her voice.

That was the lesson that Evelyn, a former student who is now a second-year in college, learned from the heated debates she had with her mother on the car ride home from school. Her story tumbled out over coffee one Sunday morning, when we met at a local café to discuss how to navigate the application process for summer jobs. Evelyn was also excited to let me know how her classes were going—especially a political science elective where she'd been the only first-year and one of only two girls, but where she was recognized by the professor for her active and thoughtful participation.

"Why do you think you're so good at speaking up, especially in a class full of senior boys?" I asked, curious whether a moment at home, at school, or even on the neighbourhood playground would jump to her mind. "Was there anything, when you were a kid, that helped you learn to be assertive in this way?"

"I'd get in the car and my mum would ask about my day," Evelyn shared, her voice picking up speed as she recalled those car rides, as if she were once again on the way home from middle school. "I would bring up a current events topic we discussed in class, and we'd fight about it for hours. I would even cry! And my mum would get upset.

"But she treated my ideas as something worth fighting about ... I learned it was good to be outspoken."

Evelyn paused, momentarily introspective, before continuing.

"Now, at college, I make a conscious decision on my first day in a new class to say something. So that I am heard. After that, it doesn't matter as much... But I want to talk and assert myself from the start."

Finding ways to help your daughter practise the basic art of speaking up should also include adults she doesn't know—that is, adults outside school and your home. For example, who orders when your family is at a local restaurant or places the call for takeaway food? These are seemingly innocuous exchanges that, for speed and convenience, most parents handle reflexively or that we now do online, without a thought. But consider whether they could be used as safe—and relatively easy to arrange, from a parent's perspective—moments for your girl to practise using her voice. Consider giving your daughter responsibility for placing the dinner order for the entire family (via the phone, not the internet or your smartphone app!), or when you visit a museum, amusement park, or hotel, ask your daughter to speak to the concierge or desk attendant—to ask a question, give feedback about something during your visit, or perhaps provide a suggestion. The details aren't important, and the context doesn't really matter. But for many girls, particularly in primary school, these are among the first instances in which they are pushed out of their comfort zone to test the power of their voices outside the home. For both introverted and extroverted children, these real-world moments are essential proving grounds for how to assert yourself confidently and respectfully. In the process, young girls learn how and when to speak up and begin to grasp the power of engaging the wider world on their own.

Jocelyn can recall specifically when her father began using this approach whenever the family called to order pizza. Rather than her twin brother—or her mum, for that matter—it was Jocelyn who had to place the order. "When I was little, I could never pick up the phone to call people I didn't know. Even to order pizza," Jocelyn admitted. "My dad would make me place the order, even though I didn't want to. Now I can do it easily."

As your daughter gets older, entering middle school or starting high school, also consider how and when you get involved in helping solve the routine problems that will no doubt crop up, in and out of school. Perhaps she's struggling in class and is upset after a particularly bad exam? This is a good chance to restrain your natural impulse to jump in; instead, try coaching your daughter on how to schedule time with and ask for help from her teacher. Suppose she is fighting with a friend on social media and it's time for the school counsellor or another adult to get involved? This is another chance to check your urge to quickly step in; instead, talk with your girl about the people at school she could turn to for assistance and talk through what else she could do to resolve the dispute herself. Or when she's offered her first job, but the hours won't work with her sports schedule? This is another opportunity to empower your girl and give her the guidance to handle the next steps, whether it's outreach to the coach or her first boss. Each of these moments may feel like a time to immediately get directly involved, but conflict, struggle, and adversity are natural opportunities for parents to take a step back and let our girls practise asserting themselves. Learn to advise and quietly support your daughter while resisting the urge to actively intercede.

In fact, to help your daughter practise acts of self-advocacy, consider creating "rules of the road" for when, how, and even if you intervene on her behalf, particularly when there are ways she can safely handle it herself. Perhaps you decide to always wait forty-eight hours before jumping in—long enough for many issues that feel urgent to a pre-teenage girl to resolve themselves or for your daughter to figure things out on her own. Or you decide that for a particular set of issues—for example, those related to a sports team or after-school activity, or those related to a specific class or teacher—you will use a rule of three. That is, you won't get involved until the third time an issue crops up. While these sorts of guideposts won't always apply, they help remind both parent and child that every situation isn't an emergency requiring Mum or Dad to step in—and most important, that our girls should be given the time, space, and support to practise self-advocating whenever possible.

Once again, Jocelyn provides a helpful illustration of this coaching-from-the-sidelines approach in action. "I was in Year 8, and I was doing terribly in maths. I can remember coming home crying more than once," she confides. Jocelyn's hands flutter while she talks, as she toys with the dozen colourful string bracelets decorating each wrist.

"I wanted my parents to help. To talk to the teacher for me. But they refused. My dad would tell me every day that he wasn't going to email my teacher for me. That I had to talk to the teacher myself."

Jocelyn paused, pursing her lips. I could see her mentally picturing the heated exchange in her kitchen five years prior. It clearly was a difficult time for both her and her parents.

"Finally, one day I went and spoke to the teacher. It helped, so I went again. And again... Now I do it all the time. And my parents just give me little reminders that I have to do these things by myself."

These rules of the road also suggest that perhaps our role as trusted adults isn't to intercede and make our girl's path to success a smooth one but instead to guide her—not just on *when* to express herself but also on *how* she shares her ideas, so that she becomes the most effective self-advocate possible. This is where combining research about common roadblocks to women's self-advocacy with your own personal stories can be incredibly powerful. The aim is to ensure your girl not only appreciates the power of her voice but also discovers natural ways to use her voice to maximum effect.

For example, do you notice that your daughter uses speech patterns that undermine what she's saying and diminish her ability to be respectfully but confidently assertive? When she starts a sentence, does she apologize when no apology is warranted ("Sorry, but...")? Or does she ask for permission to jump into the conversation ("Can I ask a question?") or otherwise qualify what she's about to say ("This may sound dumb...")? Research shows that by and large these are feminine conversational habits. That is, they are ways of speaking that many women adopt, over time, to soften our style of communication. In many cases, this approach reflects a desire to demonstrate empathy or to be non-threatening. But it's also, for many of us, an unconscious practice that comes with serious downsides. Even the female Supreme Court justices we discussed earlier were shown to routinely soften their speech by framing questions with polite openings like "May I ask" or "Excuse me"; unfortunately, this conversational habit allowed other justices the chance to interrupt before their questions were addressed.

This speaking style is also one that young girls often adopt when they unconsciously mirror the speech patterns of friends and family. While this style of communication can be useful, it should be deployed by choice, not as an involuntary reflex. Particularly since these conversational habits are difficult to break later, when our girls grow into adults and may be most impacted by personal patterns that undermine any authoritative voice they try to establish at work or in other settings.

If you notice your daughter beginning to adopt one of these speech patterns, consider pointing it out to her so she's aware of it. Ask her if she realizes she's needlessly saying sorry or otherwise qualifying her words. Then try playing a game together, to address just one conversational routine that feels most unhelpful— perhaps an unconscious habit of apologizing when it's not warranted. Set up a small jar in the kitchen, and every time she catches herself unnecessarily apologizing, she puts in a penny. If she catches you doing it, you put in two! When the jar reaches a certain point, you go out for ice cream together—and talk about what happened. Over time, this light-hearted approach to self-monitoring can make a big difference.

These ideas won't all feel right, for your family or your daughter, at any one time. Instead, pick and choose styles and approaches to try as she grows up, testing what works best as she defines her personal communication style and way of being.

What Girls Need

Even seemingly small moments when you can support your girl's developing voice will have a long, lasting impact, helping it become a natural strength that she can call on later, whatever challenges she faces and wherever she finds herself next.

I still think about that morning in the West Wing and wonder why I didn't speak up. Could I have prepared—or been prepared—differently? What would have helped me see more clearly what I wanted to say and find the right time and the right way to say it? How could I have found my voice at such an important personal and professional moment?

Fortunately, the disappointment of that day has been largely washed away by another moment with the president of the United States. An instant when I was given a chance to speak my mind—and seized the opportunity without a moment of hesitation or unconscious softening of my communication style. Backstage following a presidential speech I helped write, I was chatting with President Obama when he switched topics from the event on hand—we were there to launch a new initiative on cybersecurity—to ask about my research in Yemen and my academic work on Al-Qaeda.

More specifically, the president of the United States wondered aloud, "So, what would you do about ISIS?"

Just like that, I was having a Situation Room–worthy debate with the leader of the free world about one of the most serious national security challenges of the decade. Instantaneously, I was walking with President Obama along a winding subterranean path the Secret Service had set to get back to his motorcade, as we discussed terrorist radicalization and what social and economic pressures influence the Islamic State's recruiting efforts. I trotted to keep up with the president's rapid pace, while outlining off the top of my head a three-point plan for addressing the world's top international terrorist threat.

A few minutes later, we arrived in an underground parking lot and were standing next to the idling Beast, a heavily armoured limousine reserved for the U.S. president. Obama paused, turned to face me, and wondered aloud why I was no longer working on counterterrorism. With a smile and a handshake, I took the chance to pitch myself for a new, more senior job in national security. The president laughed and said, "One day," before shaking my hand and folding himself into the back seat of the idling limousine.

My memory of that day reminds me why, even as an adult, I have to push myself to find my voice. And why it's so important that we teach our girls to be better at self-advocating, every chance we get.

Turn Her Voice into an Influential Ask

When Joyce and Maddie bounced into my office, their broad smiles and excited energy were contagious. I couldn't help but grin. Even so, the thirteen-year-olds clutched their laptops tightly and nervously looked around the office, unsure of what to do next. I guided them to the sitting area, and as they settled in next to each other on the couch, Joyce chattered quickly while Maddie twisted her fingers and checked the chipped red paint on her nails. They were no doubt uneasy about pitching me their business proposal, which paired a love of baking with an appreciation for how much their friends would pay for cookies before lunch. They wanted to sell their baked goods at school, to earn money and test their entrepreneurial prowess. But they also knew that getting permission to do so wouldn't be an easy sell.

A few weeks prior, the girls had pitched their idea to the head of our middle school. In her soft-spoken way, Baldwin's seasoned school administrator explained the school's concerns—health regulations and allergy guidelines that limited what outside food products we sell on campus, legal and tax considerations if we provided free space to and supported an unregistered for-profit business, and questions about the optics of supporting a few students' attempt to make money off their friends and classmates, to name a few. She applauded their creativity, encouraged their enthusiasm, and then suggested alternative ideas for where and when they could sell their baked goods.

Instead, Joyce and Maddie emailed me to request a meeting. The thirteen-year-old entrepreneurs were keen to persuade the school's senior executive—and their head teacher's boss—that the benefits of their proposal outweighed any concerns. That they deserved my and the school's wholehearted support. That they had an offer worth considering.

As the two girls opened their laptops to fire up their Power-Point presentation, I was eager to hear their proposal. Not because I had any illusion that we'd likely launch their cookie company on campus, but because I wanted to see these girls in action. I wanted to watch them practise the art of persuasion and hear them negotiate. I was excited to encourage their enthusiastic and earnest attempt to get what they wanted, so they understood how important this type of ask would be for the rest of their lives.

"We think our business, Scrumptious Sweets, would help the school provide tasty treats to our friends," began Joyce, with an opening line that she'd clearly rehearsed.

She turned to Maddie, who went on with the pitch. "We

would tailor our offerings to different events at school and offer cultural desserts to get people more informed about what people in other countries eat."

Joyce finished their introductory offer with a flourish, pointing to a slide that showed blue cupcakes—our school colour—covered in colourful sprinkles. "Some of the money we raised would go to women's empowerment organizations. Because that's a thing at Baldwin and we want to support it, too."

I couldn't help but wish that I'd had such skills when I was their age. And I wondered what it would take to give every girl the chance, at school and at home, to practise the art of effective asking—to help them master the best way to pitch, influence, and negotiate so that it was second nature when they got older. When it really mattered.

During his keynote speech for the 2014 Grace Hopper Celebration of Women in Computing, then among the largest conferences for women in computer science, Microsoft's CEO was asked what advice he'd give women who felt uncomfortable requesting a raise or a promotion. What did Satya Nadella, a respected senior executive of one of the world's most powerful companies, tell a roomful of over seven thousand mostly female technologists was the most effective way to self-advocate? How did he counsel these women, who hoped to ask for what they deserved and to exert influence in an industry known for gender bias, salary gaps, and workplace discrimination?

"It's not really about asking for a raise, but knowing and

having faith that the system will give you the right raises as you go along," explained Nadella to the renowned computer scientist and college president Maria Klawe, who was moderating his talk. He went on, unabashed. "That, I think, might be one of the additional superpowers that, quite frankly, women who don't ask for a raise have. Because that's good karma."

According to one of the most powerful executives in the world—and a father of two girls—the key was for women to wait their turn and to hope and trust that the system works out. As he put it, "in the long term... things catch up."

At this point, you're likely rolling your eyes. If you're like me the first... and the second... and the third time I watched Nadella's speech, you can also feel the muscles in your shoulders tense in frustration. If you're like many of my female friends and me, you might also remember when you first realized that you were being paid less than a male colleague at work, were taking less time off than your male co-workers, or were being overlooked for a promotion or a coveted assignment because you hadn't asked to be considered. Or you recall the time you didn't ask for more help on the home front, only to be stuck juggling a last-minute request at the office that delayed your departure along with the children's complicated after-school schedule, the dog sitter who quit, and an overdue birthday present for your nephew.

If you have a young girl in your life, you're also undoubtedly wondering how to ensure that this sort of thinking doesn't continue into the next generation. How can we make sure that today's girls grow into women who understand not just how to speak up but how to effectively use their voice to influence others, in and out of the workplace? What can we do to ensure that tomorrow's leading women ask for what they need and want, and get what they deserve, personally and professionally?

▌ Why Is the Ask So Important?

No doubt, very few of us have seen "effective asker" listed on a CV or LinkedIn profile. Like many of the essential skills we'll discuss in this book, the ability to productively persuade another person, group, or organization to give you what you need or want is a skill that is often attributed to natural talent or perhaps one's personality. As a result, it's not something that many people think to nurture in themselves or focus on for our girls—despite the fact that a knack for asking (and getting!) is so crucial to success, whether you're employed at a large company, trying to get a small business off the ground, working part time, navigating the complicated realities of being a stay-at-home parent, negotiating the terms of your first flat lease, buying a car, or trying to get the support your daughter needs at school.

When we consider what our children's future looks like, it becomes clear that the ability to ask effectively will be even more critical in decades to come. Not only are the nature of work and types of jobs people will have evolving, but the structures that define work are changing, too. Today's youngest workers change jobs more often than previous generations, with most switching positions and companies four times in the first ten years after university. For comparison, those of us born from the 1960s to the 1980s average only two job changes before turning thirty-two years old. And women appear to job-hop more than men. Meanwhile, more and more young people aspire to be independent entrepreneurs: 77 per cent of students in middle and senior school want to be their own boss one day, and 45 per cent want to start their own business. The children of Generation Z, which includes girls and boys born after 1995, are considered among the most entrepreneurial, and recent studies confirm a higher rate of what's called entrepreneurial intention, or seeing yourself as a likely entrepreneur, among this younger generation. As a result of this changing outlook in the next generation of workers, companies have started to alter how they recruit, retain, and reward talent—offering things like flexitime, student loan repayment, overseas assignments, or other creative benefits for those who ask effectively.

The combined growing influences of a shifting job market, historically non-traditional forms of work, and more personalized approaches to compensating performance add a new layer of complication for young women not skilled at negotiating. But if we prepare them correctly, a talent for asking and persuading can be a critical aspect of how they thrive in the new landscape of the professional world.

What's more, as technology and globalization make the world even more interconnected and as the future of work demands greater entrepreneurial skills, "success" will be determined more and more by your ability to advocate effectively for yourself and productively influence those in your personal and professional network. The ability to persuade and negotiate will become increasingly vital, and a talent for asking effectively will become a core differentiator, whether you're in a junior or a senior role. For jobs in many of the industries that today's school-aged kids admire, including in technology and as an entrepreneur, being persuasive is essential for success. This is the adult world awaiting today's kids.

In fact, the fundamental soft skills that translate into a talented "asker" are already at the top of the list of what employers want most in new recruits. When the National Association of Colleges and Employers in the U.S. surveyed companies about what they look for in a candidate's CV, more than two-thirds said they prioritized skills like written and verbal communication, leadership, initiative, and the ability to work in a team—all elements core to those who can effectively persuade others and ask for what they need. Meanwhile, skills like tactfulness, friendliness, and, perhaps surprisingly, fluency in a foreign language were at the bottom of the wish list.

This vision of our girls' future is further complicated by the unavoidable realities facing young women who want both a career and a family when they grow up. Studies show that more women aspire not just to find a fulfilling job but to ambitiously pursue leadership roles in their chosen industry. In PwC's 2018 survey of 3,637 professional women from sixty-one countries around the world and across industries, 75 per cent said that getting to the top of their career and reaching a leadership position is important, and 82 per cent felt confident in their ability to fulfil their career objectives. Even so, 42 per cent felt "nervous" about how having children would impact their career, while 48 per cent of new mothers felt "overlooked" for promotions and special projects; those numbers jumped to 53 and 63 per cent, respectively, for women who self-identify as minorities.

As we encourage our girls to imagine their own most success-ful personal and professional adult selves, we must also give them the skills they need to advocate for themselves effectively and navigate the compromises that will have to be made, at work and at home, to thrive in multiple spheres of life. There is no magic wand to help them achieve work–life balance—particularly, as any mother who works outside the home will admit, the Zen-like picture of work–life balance that seems possible only in a Holly-wood movie. Almost any life that our young girls imagine will come with natural tensions between the personal and the profes-sional. As we talk about this reality more openly with young women, we also need to make sure they are prepared to navigate the difficult moments they'll no doubt face. That will make it all the more critical for girls to ask for what they need in their per-sonal lives, too.

Alarmingly, studies indicate that the effective ask still eludes many women. Forty-four per cent of professional women expect to be approached by their boss for a promotion, 39 per cent would go for that more senior job only if they met all the criteria for the role, and a mere 17 per cent would ask for a promotion if they met some but not all of the job requirements. I've seen how these statistics play out in everyday life. I still groan inwardly when I remember finding out, after the fact, that I'd accepted a job at a lower starting salary than my male peers at the Pentagon, despite a graduate degree and years of active duty experience in the military. And I can't help the sigh that escapes me when I recall the story of Nikki, a final-year student at my school who thought she was being underpaid at her summer job but didn't know what to do about it. Like me, she hadn't been taught to ask for what she deserved.

What if we teach our girls early on how to turn their voice into a powerful ask and use their own style of influence to maximum effect? What if we could help ensure that today's young women don't have to wait for "good karma" to come their way?

As we took our seats in the austere conference room, Alan, my boss, subtly gestured to his right, indicating that I should sit at the centre of the gleaming mahogany conference table. He settled into the chair to my left, while our colleague from the State Department unpacked his briefcase to my right. The table could fit at least twenty people, so a half-dozen plush leather chairs sat empty to either side of us. I sank into the deep bucket seat and, with my feet not quite hitting the ground, felt the chair swivel from side to side. I quickly scooted to the edge of the chair to stop the spinning before anyone noticed.

Our German counterparts manoeuvred to the other side of the oversize table that floated in the centre of a mostly empty room. The chief of mission looked to his left and right, mentally calculating where to sit. His three colleagues, representing his country's foreign ministry, defence ministry, and intelligence community, chatted amicably about the weather, patiently waiting for their boss to choose his seat. A bird flew past the floor-to-ceiling windows that flanked three sides of the room, prompting me to momentarily appreciate our view of the thick trees that soared above the embassy and blocked any view from the nearby street. The windowpanes were no doubt made with special glass that shielded attempts to electronically eavesdrop on the diplomatic negotiations that regularly went on in the room.

As I pulled from my handbag a standard government-issue notebook and pen and placed them on the table, the chief of mission settled into the seat directly across from me—at the centre of the table, the most "senior" position.

For the next hour and a half, we discussed the fate of a young man held in U.S. custody at the Defense Department's detention centre in Guantánamo Bay, Cuba. The conversation bobbed and weaved as we danced between topics—reviewing the detainee's background, the intelligence reports about his actions in the global war on terror, and the documentation regarding his ties to Germany, where the young man had residency status and family connections. We covered the U.S. government's security concerns and the humanitarian laws governing his treatment.

The meeting lasted long enough for my feet to fall asleep beneath the chair. Questions remained about whether this detainee would be released into German custody and repatriated to Germany, but major headway had been made. Given recent news about German chancellor Angela Merkel's interest in the case, I had no doubt that a report would be drafted as soon as we walked out of the room to update diplomats in Berlin on the progress of our discussions.

Turn Her Voice into an Influential Ask

As our car crossed Memorial Bridge on the way back to the Pentagon, Alan smiled broadly and offered hearty congratulations for a job well done. Then he paused, looking out his window at the entrance of Arlington National Cemetery before continuing, "Do you know why I had you sit in the middle?"

"You didn't want to sit next to Steve," I teased, alluding to our colleague from the Department of State. Long-standing friendly competition between government agencies meant that we regularly joked about our State Department counterparts.

"It's a trick I learned from negotiating with the North Koreans. If you sat in the centre, the Germans would be thrown off."

"Huh?" I asked, utterly confused.

"Most men aren't used to negotiating with a woman. Especially a young woman," Alan continued. "I knew they'd want to defer to you. It's a cultural norm that would be hard to resist. Did you notice that they directed their questions first to you? That they waited for you to respond, then looked my way for validation?"

I shrugged, but in my mind's eye, I could picture the chief of mission doing just that.

"While they were watching you, I was watching them. I gauged their reactions as you outlined our asks. It helped me figure out whether we were persuading them to accept our terms."

For the first time, I realized that "negotiating" could be a gendered term. And that how my gender was perceived could be an advantage, too.

▌Is Asking Really Different for Women and Men?

Julissa's booming voice enters a room ten seconds before she does. Her energy matches her physical presence, right down to her colourful outfits and four-inch heels.

As the former president of a conglomerate of thirteen Telemundo television stations and three radio stations, and as the current senior executive charged with overseeing all of the Smithsonian's communications and external affairs, Julissa Marenco knows how to use her voice. She knows how to successfully lead in mostly male-dominated workplaces, including as the only woman and only minority on her current organization's senior executive staff.

She also understands the subtle and not-so-subtle differences between expressing herself and asking for—and getting—what she needs and deserves. And she has seen women, throughout her career, struggle with this difference.

"I think women, generally speaking, can be their own worst enemy," Julissa candidly shared during our long overdue catch-up call. She went on to describe the countless meetings she's sat through where women didn't ask for what they deserved—in particular, when they let their compensation aspirations be overlooked.

"It shocked me to see that, every time, the women didn't talk about what they needed," she explained. "The men did, every day. They would always say 'I deserve this, I merit that.' The women stayed silent."

Turn Her Voice into an Influential Ask

She also confessed that, even after gaining years of experience and steadily earning more senior roles and responsibilities, she still reverts to her "twenty-year-old self" sometimes. "I still occasionally think *thank you for having me* when offered a project or promotion."

Julissa paused mid-thought and sighed deeply, clearly remembering a recent moment when she didn't ask for what she deserved. "I think we underestimate ourselves."

Research shows that Julissa's experience mirrors that of millions of women around the world. By and large, we are less adept at asking for what we want and deserve, whether we're negotiating for a salary or promotion, a car, or help on the home front. Women often don't get what they want because we don't ask for it, and when we do negotiate, the outcomes for us aren't as good as they are for men.

This reality has been confirmed time and again by social scientists and researchers who explore the art of asking. The study of negotiation has been ongoing for centuries, reflecting the natural fact that every person will negotiate at some point in life and also academic interest in conflict management and treaty negotiation that grew out of multiple world wars. But the focus on how aspects of your identity, including gender, race, and social status, impact your ability to successfully ask began relatively recently. In 1995, two legal scholars interested in bargaining strategies dived headlong into the fray, hoping to figure out whether gender or race gave you an advantage when buying a new car. Ian Ayres and Peter Siegelman trained thirty-eight women and men to haggle for a car, following a set script that outlined how—and even how quickly—negotiations should unfold, and then sent them to 153 dealerships across Chicago to test their asking prowess. Every prospective car buyer was around thirty years old, plus or minus two years, with similar levels of education. They were also screened for "average" attractiveness, instructed to wear yuppie clothing, and coached on how to describe their jobs in similarly bland terms. There were never so many "systems analysts at a large bank" looking for a car at the same time.

What unfolded during 306 visits to dealerships scattered around Chicago was a series of individual car negotiations that ultimately ended with the tester telling the salesperson, "Thanks, but I need to think about this before I make up my mind." The prospective car buyers would then report to the two researchers, based at Yale Law School and the Chicago-based American Bar Foundation, details like the initial asking price, the final sales price, and the length of each negotiation.

The study's results were astounding and clearly demonstrated how gender impacts negotiations, with a level of statistical significance that overcame any doubts about the testers' natural or learned differences in negotiating ability. Car dealers quoted women and black customers significantly higher prices for the same car, even though all the customers were trained to use identical ask strategies and follow a uniform negotiating script. White men got the best deal—both initially and in the final offer. White women were initially asked to pay, on average, about $110 more than their white male counterparts. Black women were asked to pay about $320 more. Even after the process of negotiating lowered the dealers' offer, women were still asked to pay, on average, between $92 and $410 more than a white male. All for the same car.

What's more, in at least 40 per cent of the cases, a white male buyer received an initial offer—that is, the starting price without any negotiating—that was a better price (lower!) than what a woman or minority customer would receive after about forty-five minutes of asking for a discount. Whether they bargained hard or not at all, women were at a disadvantage, and minority women even more so.

The scholars concluded that being a woman or minority was used as a proxy for how much less one would be willing to settle for. For car dealers, at least, "sucker" was a gendered term.

Now I bet you're wondering if the story would play out this way at your local car dealership today. How much has changed in the past twenty years?

Let's see what happens if we focus on cars for a few moments longer. Echoing Ayres and Siegelman's car dealership test, a team of professors from Northwestern's Kellogg School of Management and Harvard Business School developed an experiment to study how gender and other factors affect the price of a standard car repair. Over sixteen weeks in the summer and autumn of 2012, nine women and men called nearly 2,800 repair shops around the United States to ask how much it would cost to fix a broken radiator on a Toyota Camry. They recorded over 4,600 quotes for what should have been a $365 (£280) repair job. The female askers were given prices, on average, nearly $23 (£18) over prices that men were quoted. Apparently, not much has changed.

But what happens if we test the influence of one's gender on negotiations more broadly? Are women considered an easy mark in other markets, too? Are today's female bargainers better than our predecessors?

Unfortunately, research over the past two decades validates that we should still be concerned about the disadvantages facing women making an ask. It's more than just a bias in the auto industry that hampers women from effectively asking for what they need and deserve.

Among the most influential works on this issue was one published in 2003 by Linda Babcock and Sara Laschever, who explored a range of societal and psychological reasons that inhibit most women from asking. As their research and subsequent book *Women Don't Ask* argued, women's reluctance is a learned behaviour based on social conditioning and reflects a number of unwritten norms—including a tendency to see negotiation as a "masculine" act, the backlash women often face when they do ask, and the fact that women typically have smaller professional networks and lack the information necessary to make a "good" ask. As a result, they avoid the process from the start.

One survey Babcock and Laschever conducted with recent graduates from Carnegie Mellon University showed that when searching for their first job after graduate school, men were eight times more likely than women to negotiate their starting salary. Despite advice from the university's careers advice office, which told all its students to negotiate their job offers, a mere 7 per cent of the women asked for more money than they were initially offered. For comparison, 57 per cent of the male graduate students countered their opening salary offer—and were rewarded with starting salaries that were over $4,000 (or 7.4 per cent) higher than those of their female peers.

The same results held true in other studies, too. Take the controlled laboratory experiment in which seventy-four people played the word game Boggle for a cash reward of anywhere from $3 to $10. At the end of the game, the players were handed the lowest cash payment and asked, "Is three dollars okay?" Each participant simply had to ask for more money to be given the full $10 reward. The men were eight times more likely than women to ask for more money. And although both a female and male research assistant supervised the game and handed out the money, only the woman was asked to up the reward. Women were both significantly less likely to ask—and significantly more likely to *be* asked, based on participants' reactions when the female research assistant was presiding.

Or consider the study by two economists, John List of the University of Chicago and Andreas Leibbrandt of Australia's Monash University, known for using field experiments to explore how microeconomic theories impact the real world. Turning their attention to the influence of gender on pay differences, they created a natural experiment involving approximately 2,500 women and men looking for work via online employment postings. Eighteen administrative assistant positions were posted on job sites aimed at people seeking work in nine cities around the United States. As was the case in other similar job listings, the position called for candidates "comfortable with typical administrative duties—light correspondence, proofreading, filing, email, and phone communication" and listed an hourly compensation.

What Girls Need

For the 2,422 applicants, of whom about two-thirds were women, researchers screened the interviews to determine whether or not people asked for a higher wage or indicated that they were willing to work for less. Echoing the findings of other studies, when a job description did not clearly advertise that wages were negotiable, women were found to be less likely to demand more money and more likely to indicate they'd be willing to work for a lower wage. Unless they were explicitly told to bargain, in which case the gender gap disappeared.

The impact of this reluctance to negotiate is lasting and significant, and it sets the stage for continued gender-based disparities for years to come. In other words, it impedes young women's progress before they've even started. It's not simply the fact that the wages forfeited in one year could cover a few months' worth of childcare, make a nice dent in student loan debt, or provide a healthy influx to an early retirement account. More critically, employees who don't negotiate their first salary lose approximately half a million dollars over the course of their career, as a result of the compound effect of any raises, bonuses, or wage increases due to job changes that were benchmarked on that lower starting salary.

Of course, the impact of gender on the efficacy of one's negotiating prowess isn't just seen at car dealerships and on the job market. Other research has determined what happens when women negotiate online, shielded by the anonymity and gender blindness of the internet, when women negotiate against men as opposed to someone of their own gender, and when female athletes negotiate. There have also been studies about how negotiations typically play out in matriarchal versus patriarchal communities, and how the item being negotiated for impacts performance. According to this last eyebrow-raising study, women and men are equally effective when negotiating for perceived "feminine" products, like glass beads, but men negotiate more effectively for "masculine" things, like car headlights.

In other words, women are likely to see versions of the car dealership experiment play out in the real world, at critical junctures and over the course of their lifetimes. Take a recent study on the salary gap in Australia, where women's average full-time pay is 13.9 per cent less than that of men. Researchers screened a database of 4,600 workers, just over half of whom were women, from 840 different employers to determine whether people had "attempted to attain a better wage". It turns out that 66 per cent of the women—as compared with 75 per cent of the men—had asked for a raise in pay. Apparently, women (in Australia, at least) were beginning to ask at nearly the same rate as men. But when asked about the outcomes of these negotiations, the women were less likely to report success; of those surveyed, women were a fourth less likely to have gotten a raise.

What's happening here? One rationale explored by researchers is that women are penalized for adopting what's perceived as a "masculine" tendency to ask for what they want. In one study of the social costs associated with negotiating, 119 university students, most of whom were in their early twenties, role-played managers hiring summer interns—a handful of whom were instructed to negotiate for salary and benefits. The female candidates were penalized harshly for initiating negotiations. While evaluators were less likely to hire any woman or man who negotiated, the negative effect on women was twice as large as for men. A follow-up experiment to judge a candidate's perceived "likeability" after negotiating revealed a clear backlash against women who asked. Evaluators rated the women who negotiated as too demanding and not nice, but there was no major impact on the perceptions of male negotiators; the negative social effect overall was 5.5 times greater for women than men. As this scenario repeats itself over time, women learn that their requests are poorly received and come at a social cost, and begin to avoid asking when it counts most.

The system may be (slowly) changing, but there's still a double standard at play. Women are penalized for negotiating in the same way as men. In other words, we can't simply encourage our girls to speak up more. We also need to teach them how to ask effectively.

No matter how you look at it, our girls have a problem getting what they need and deserve. Even in an era when women are touted for breaking gender stereotypes, women still admit to having less confidence in their skills of persuasion, concede feeling more anxiety about the process of negotiating than their male counterparts, and don't see the strong results their male peers do.

All too often, this means that women avoid asking for what they need. And when women ask, they don't receive. Which is a problem. Not just for women, but for girls and those who love them.

After women (and men) around the world condemned Satya Nadella's suggestion from the stage of the Grace Hopper Celebration that women shouldn't bother to negotiate, Nadella issued a statement saying that he "answered that question completely wrong" and that his advice to women who aren't comfortable asking for the compensation they deserve was off the mark. Upon reflection, he suggested that women should ask for a raise if they feel they deserve one. And in a message sent out via social media, he noted that the tech industry, as a whole, must also do its part to help even the playing field for women.

Four years later, the Microsoft CEO was again asked to revisit the advice he gave women who feel uncomfortable asking in workplaces like the tech industry, where gender biases have been the historic norm. After admitting the ridiculousness of his original response, Nadella encouraged women to "advocate for themselves. They should find other allies, male or female, who can advocate for them. And make sure that they don't accept status quo."

He's right, of course. At least in part.

Even as the system must change to better address workplace bias—Nadella was clear on this aspect—women can do more to help themselves along the way. He missed the fact that it's important to train girls, when they're young, in this approach. It's too late to play catch-up when they finally arrive at Microsoft.

What's a Parent to Do?

Fortunately, there are things we can do to ensure that girls are prepared for these realities. Along with helping school-aged girls learn to speak out and voice their opinion, we must also ensure that each one understands how to use her voice in the most influential way possible—not just to express her thoughts and ideas but to get what she needs, in work and in life. This means not only encouraging your daughter to hold fast to every child's natural tendency to ask questions but, as she grows up, helping her practise asking for things effectively in the supportive sanctuary of home or with family, and in more uncomfortable situations, too. In doing so, she will learn the art of persuasion, the skills to negotiate, and ways to use these talents to her advantage later on, when it really counts.

▊ Endless Asks Can Be a Good Thing

As any parent knows, kids are naturally predisposed to asking questions. A ton of them. Studies show that by age four, both girls and boys ask about a hundred questions a day. Any reader who's recently gone through this phase likely has personal stories that attest to this fact—and can recall the time when you reached your breaking point after hearing that hundredth (or thousandth?) "why" from your child. Even when we know asking questions is good for children because it encourages their innate curiosity and helps them learn, most of us can recall a time when we hit our breaking point and hoped that the endless asks would stop.

Studies suggest that children's natural inclination to ask questions—and ask a lot of them—wanes in primary school. And pretty much stops by middle school, right around the time that one-word answers from our pre-teenagers become the norm. That natural impetus to ask and alongside it, the moments of regular, albeit immature, attempts to persuade others to give you what you want, is lost over time. Not least because, as Richard Saul Wurman, the architect and graphic designer renowned for creating the TED conference, noted, "In school, we're rewarded for having the answer, not for asking a good question." Formal systems of school often prioritize structured models of communication and feedback, including via tests, grades, and report cards, dampening kids' tendency to ask and, in many cases, to directly self-advocate. Particularly girls. Even the talkative ones. Especially the quiet ones.

The key is to cultivate curiosity and self-advocacy as your daughter's natural inclination may otherwise begin to fade. To find small everyday ways in which you can encourage your daughter to practise the act of asking, and just as critical, the follow-up step of persuading when the answer to the original request is no.

Yes, I know. At first it sounds like a lot of exhausting work to engage in a debate every time your daughter wants to download another app on your phone or watch one more episode of her favourite cartoon. The trick is to place this approach within the context of regular parenting routines. It doesn't have to be a weekly occurrence—or drive you crazy—to make a difference. Instead, consider how to strategically deploy this tactic in moments that really matter for your girl. What are the times that constitute, in your family, the teenage equivalent of that big raise she'll deserve as an adult or an important concession she'll want from her future partner? Choose to dig into those discussions.

The next time your daughter asks for something big—a special toy or privilege, like a sleepover on a school night or a change to her curfew—make her persuade you, and think through her request and the context in which it fits into your family. Even if you've already decided to agree with the ask, have her share three reasons why her request deserves your support. And consider formalizing the process a bit. Ask her to come back in a day (or a week), and persuade you that she deserves whatever "important" thing is on her mind. Remind her that a good pitch includes some research and a solid rationale, then see what she comes up with.

The outcome of her effort isn't critical, so there's no need to change your decision. The key is to have her pause and take notice of those moments when she wants to feel heard, and then use the opportunity to help her practise asking. Indeed, research has shown that experience in negotiating significantly helps women, when they're adults, do better on subsequent negotiations; perhaps not surprisingly, practice really does have a major impact. The crucial step is not to wait until our girls are adults to have them start practising. Regardless of the outcome of her ask, also provide your daughter with feedback about the most and least convincing aspects of her pitch. Did she communicate well and explain what she wanted clearly? Was she more persuasive when she used facts, stories, or something else? Did she get emotional or angry, or was she calm—and in either case, did she manage her emotions to maximum effect? Positive reinforcement is essential to affirm that you applaud her self-advocacy.

One of the most memorable times I saw this approach in action was during a recent holiday, when I joined my family and their friends for a large sit-down home-cooked dinner—the sort that included multiple courses, linen napkins, and more than one dessert option. That night, the guests included Jordan, a Philadelphia-area talent manager, and his two school-aged girls. Throughout dinner, Anna, his elder daughter, was surreptitiously checking her phone under the table, messaging friends and checking social media. Her covert texting lasted until just before dessert, when Jordan decided enough was enough, reminded her of the "no phone at dinner" rule, and confiscated her iPhone for the night. Like any teenager, Anna tried to defend herself. Then she sulked. Then she turned to her little sister, Callie, and began badgering her; baiting her younger sibling was a suitable alternative to the entertainment of clandestine peeks at TikTok.

Rather than allow the brewing fight to unfold, Jordan turned the tables on his daughters and had them partner to advocate for Anna's "right" to her smartphone. He offered to consider returning the phone sooner if Callie made a good case for it by the end of dinner. While Jordan freely admits he used this tactic as a diversion more than anything else, the result was a textbook example of how to help his girls practise their ask and learn the power of persuasive self-advocacy in a safe and supportive environment.

Twelve-year-old Callie, the shyer of the two girls, spent the next fifteen minutes crafting her argument. And Anna stopped teasing her, instead feeding her younger sister ideas that might help win back the iPhone. As we adults finished our coffee, Callie stood to present her three-point argument to the table— masterfully explaining the social and educational reasons why her sister needed her phone back as soon as possible. Her rationale may not have held up under Supreme Court review, but her calm, thoughtful, and convincing case was an excellent real-life demonstration of how important it is to give our girls the chance to practise persuasion. It also supported research that shows the importance of role-playing for negotiators and that girls ask more effectively when advocating for someone else. Jordan even decided to let Anna have her phone back for the car ride home.

Jordan's experience shows us that even though adding a new project to the daily to-do list of parenting may seem overwhelming, you can actually easily integrate your girl's practice of self-advocacy skills into your family's routine. And it doesn't just have to be your daughter asking for herself. Have her practise asking for her sister, brother, or another family member. Or consider what other things your daughter cares about, outside home and daily life, and find ways to help her ask for them.

Early Steps to Becoming a Persuasive Adult

When Kate entered middle school, animals and the environment became her favourite topics of discussion. She read blogs about environmental protection efforts online, talked about the subject endlessly, and followed animal rights groups on Instagram. She also started to get serious about recycling at home, constantly reminding her mum that the soft drinks cans needed to be washed before being put into the recycling bin and even suggesting they start to compost.

Turn Her Voice into an Influential Ask

By the time she hit Year 9, she was focused on what was going on at school—and started to have serious concerns about how we handled recycling and waste around Baldwin's campus. In particular, she was upset that we still had plastic straws in the dining hall.

Before long, she started emailing our school's head of dining services and director of facilities, asking why we still had straws, outlining her research on why plastic straws were bad for the environment, and suggesting economic advantages if the school stopped buying straws. When she didn't hear back, she emailed my assistant to make sure the issue was flagged for my attention and to ask for a meeting about her request to remove straws from our dining hall.

Kate had found a reason to bargain for something she wanted, to advocate in a certain way that didn't just require raising her voice but also meant asking for something specific. Research shows that women are more apt to ask when they're advocating on behalf of someone or something else. Kate's advocacy was proof of that—plus her passion gave her the chance to work on her skills of persuasion.

But what if your daughter is shy? What if reaching out for a meeting with her head teacher or other adult wouldn't feel right?

You might follow the example of Beth, a parent of three young kids whose ten-year-old daughter, Savannah, was begging for a hedgehog. In the course of hunting for just the right hedgehog, they discovered that it's actually illegal in Pennsylvania to keep this small animal as a pet. Rather than simply saying, "Sorry, not possible", or taking on the issue as another problem for her to solve, Beth instead turned to her daughter and said, "Your turn."

With a little bit of parental guidance, Savannah drafted an online petition using Change.org—a website that provides easy tools for creating free virtual petitions. With adult oversight, its resources can be great safe tools for kids to use, too. Savannah sent her appeal to as many adults as she had emails for. I am certain that the 153 people who signed the petition were mostly classmates' parents and family friends. She then sent a letter to Pennsylvania's governor and her state representative, explaining why hedgehogs should be legal as pets showing how many supporters she had for her request.

A month or so later, when she updated me on her progress, she described the response she received to her demand for a legislative fix to her hedgehog problem. It included an update from her state representative about the status of a bill that was brought forward to legalize hedgehogs as pets in Pennsylvania.

"Unfortunately, this bill did not pass," admitted Savannah, no doubt disappointed that her dreams of a pet were deterred. But she was excited that the state official said he "was proud of someone so young making this effort."

She learned the lesson that counted most: that asking matters. And she practised critical skills in how to go about influencing others and gaining support for her ideas, in a way that fits best with her quiet temperament. She was encouraged to grow comfortable with her own personalized approach to asking, which in this particular case meant emailing dozens of adults and making her case in a formal, grown-up way. The act of persuading others will no doubt be more natural to her for years to come, at home and in any future work environment.

At my school, we even create formal, age-appropriate systems to help our students consciously practise the art of asking and develop their personal negotiating style. For example, early each spring, the senior class officially petitions all our teachers to gain extra privileges before graduation. After much debate about what requests will likely be well received and how they can most effectively pitch their wish list, the class officers attend a faculty meeting to present their demands. It's a wish list that typically includes the standard teenage requests—more days when they don't have to adhere to our dress code, the chance to leave campus during the school day, the opportunity to cut class, and a request for their favourite foods in the cafeteria.

What unfolds is a wonderful case study in creative and effective persuasion. The girls begin by trying to set a tone of partnership. The week prior to their official in-person ask, the students leave notes for their teachers, thanking them for all they do. They bake cookies for the faculty lounge and find ways to help out around campus. Then the day of the faculty meeting, four teenage girls formally present their requests and outline the rationale for each demand. Creativity counts, as does their ability to convince a roomful of their teachers why each ask is mutually beneficial for the girls and the school.

Unbeknown to the girls, the upper school head reviews the list in advance to determine which asks make sense. Most years, the girls get a standard assortment of additional free time, more time without a dress code, and extra days of tater tots and waffles on the lunch menu. The girls cheer for whatever privileges they receive and, in the remaining few weeks of school, revel in those requests that are fulfilled and are too distracted to notice those asks that aren't as successful.

While the excitement of these small wins sticks out in the moment, what has the most lasting impact is that they practise learning how to craft influential asks. That they think through the art of persuading. That the adults in their lives reaffirm how important it is to find appropriate and effective ways to demand what you want and negotiate for what you need.

What About Those Problematic Salary Negotiations?

Although every negotiation your girl faces as an adult won't involve wages or money, the gender-based salary gap remains one of the hardest hurdles for women to overcome, even in countries that have had equal pay legislation for many years. What's more, salary and personalized benefit negotiations will be an even more important part of our children's future work experience than they are today. They will change jobs more often than any previous generation and navigate ever more flexible work situations, including working from home, working part time, and consultancy-oriented work. All of this will require more frequently negotiating their salary, title, benefits, roles, and responsibilities.

While efforts are under way to fix systems that perpetuate gender-based wage disparities, changing entrenched societal norms and customs is a slow process. Even as that systemic work continues and requires active support, we must also spend time preparing our girls for the wage biases that will likely remain the reality for the foreseeable future.

As is true of almost all of the issues we'll discuss in this book, a critical piece of tackling the problem is finding ways to talk about the issue openly, in an age-appropriate way, with our girls—and not to shy away from telling them about our own personal experience, even when our story doesn't illustrate an ideal scenario. While these may not be obvious conversations when your daughter is young, there are easy ways to ensure negotiating does not become a taboo subject for our girls.

Think about it the next time you choose a board game for family night. Why not pick a classic negotiations game like Diplomacy or Catan (or Catan Junior, for younger kids), which teach basic skills of negotiation in a way that's fun for all ages? Catan, formerly called Settlers of Catan, is an especially engaging way to help your girl practise the art of negotiating—and for her to realize that money isn't an off-limits subject. Playing these games allows you to start a conversation, in a relaxed way, about how to ask for what you want or think you deserve, and to talk about the often uncomfortable subject of money.

Or consider how you respond the next time your daughter mentions her interest in the school play, a specific position on the football team, or a role in a club or activity at school. Talk with her about what attributes are ideal for the role—and then describe how important it is to try out, regardless of whether she has all those skills or qualities. Cementing in young girls' minds that even if they don't have every skill in the job profile they should still apply will make it more natural for them to apply for that "stretch job" one day. The one that all of their male friends are applying for, even those who are underqualified.

At the very least, when your girl applies for her first job, make sure she knows to do some research in advance about the expectations and likely salary. And that she knows to ask, in a respectful way, "I understand that the going salary rate is x. What are you offering? Is there any room to negotiate?" For that first job, as a summer camp counsellor or at the local pizza place, there will no doubt be very little room for negotiating. That's okay. Once again, the outcome doesn't matter. Just the fact that she practises the steps of an effective ask, in the context of salary and wages, will give her an advantage down the line when there is room to negotiate. The key to ensure she doesn't internalize the unspoken message that negotiating and persuading are "not something girls do".

That was the approach taken by Nikki, the final-year student I mentioned earlier, who was being underpaid at her summer job but didn't know what to do. A friend suggested she seek advice from an adult, so the seventeen-year-old talked it through with a staff member at school—the security guard with a friendly smile she saw wandering the halls each day. He encouraged her to approach the manager of the summer camp where she worked and coached her on what to say. A few days later, Nikki went to her boss and formally outlined why she was concerned about her pay. She mentioned research she'd found online about what camp counsellors were paid in the area.

Thanks to that ask, she got an extra paycheque before the

summer was done. It turns out she and her friends were being underpaid, unbeknown to the folks overseeing the camp. She was the first one to ask. And she got what she deserved as a result.

L et's not forget about Joyce and Maddie, who visited me at the start of this chapter in hopes of starting a cupcake company at school. As their pitch continued, the two middle school pupils managed to cover every aspect of their business in a colourful eight-slide presentation. Joyce talked about all the research they had done on permitting, describing why they couldn't get a permit but how they'd ensure that no nuts or other allergens would be sold at school. Maddie described when and where they'd sell their products, and how they'd vary their cupcake selection to include lemon, blueberry, and chocolate with caramel pastry cream flavours, but would make sure they were "delicious and healthy, too." The girls even offered to donate a portion of the proceeds from their cookie sales to the school.

As the words "Thank you!" popped onto their laptop screen, pasted over a closeup picture of a mouthwatering chocolate and vanilla cupcake, the thirteen-year-olds looked at each other and smiled so widely I could see the rubber bands in Maddie's braces. They were clearly proud of their ask.

To the girls' disappointment, they didn't get a yes—this time. Instead, I talked with them about other options for pursuing their baking business. And we discussed what they thought they did well in their pitch and what things they wanted to improve next time, how they prepared, and who helped them most.

What Girls Need

"We were nervous," Joyce admitted, "so we practised talking not so fast. And we planned out what we were each going to say."

Maddie agreed with her friend, then described the research they did on health codes and the time spent trying to explain their request in a personal way. "My parents helped me come up with the reasons why you should believe in our business. They said that these would be really important to mention."

Then the girls admitted that they did these sorts of asks all the time.

"I did a presentation when I wanted a phone," Maddie explained, "and once when we wanted to take a trip together... But also when we ask for sleepovers!"

Her long ponytail swung behind her as she excitedly leaned over her computer to find an example of another pitch presentation. Seconds later, the words "Mega Sleepover!!!!" popped onto her screen, surrounded by rainbow-coloured balloons. The slides that followed described the girls' last big ask—a sleepover on a holiday weekend—along with their priority requests: special snacks for movie night (popcorn with mini M&Ms!), the chance to bake a cake (chocolate fudge!), a movie marathon (*How to Marry a Millionaire* with a fort in the living room!), and specific requests for breakfast the next day (shaped pancakes and hot cocoa with pretty marshmallows!).

Joyce and Maddie got a yes from their parents for their sleepover request. For now, that's reward enough. But I'm most excited to see what happens when, as adults, these girls ask for what they need and want.

Cultivate Her Competitive Spirit

Chloe stepped to the front of the classroom, a bundle of nervous energy mixed with a bit of fear. She unconsciously tapped her foot and twisted her long hair, which her mum had helped pull into a ponytail using a favourite purple hair tie.

It was the start of her school's geography bee, a widely publicized annual event during which students in the middle school years competed for the chance to represent their school at the statewide contest. Today's first round was during homeroom. Chloe was next in line to answer a question that would determine if she'd be one of two from her year group to progress to the next round of competition. There she would sit onstage during a whole-school assembly, answering geography questions with a handful of kids from other homerooms.

Chloe was confident. She knew every state and state capital in the country, thanks to the licence plate game she played with her mum in the car; she took great pride in being able to spell each one, even the tricky capitals like Juneau and Tallahassee. She'd reviewed her teacher's prep questions for a few weeks and had developed a knack for remembering random facts about world geography.

But Chloe hated the idea of standing up in front of her class-mates and teachers to test her knowledge against her friends. What if she got an answer wrong? That would be so embarrass-ing. Even worse, what if she got an answer right? Her friends would think she was showing off, that she wanted to beat them.

When Chloe's turn came, her friend, Emma, shot her a big smile. Then her teacher read from the sheet of questions: "Chloe, the Antietam battlefield is located in which mid-Atlantic state?"

That's an easy one, she thought. *It's Maryland, for sure.* Her family had even toured the site one summer a few years back, when she was visiting her grandparents. Chloe remembered how hot it was, and how her dad got a kick out of reading the plaques that contained odd scraps of historical information.

Chloe paused, looking at kids to her left and right who were part of that day's geography bee. Then she made a split-second decision and responded, "The Antietam battlefield is located in Virginia."

Recounting that moment in the geography bee a year later, Chloe was nonchalant about knocking herself out of the compe-tition the first chance she had. "I didn't want to stand up in front of everyone, get the wrong answer, and have my face turn red," she said with a shrug.

After a little hesitation, we started to discuss not just the geography bee but other competitions: the water balloon toss tournament at camp, a football game at school, and card games at home. "I don't want to hurt anyone's feelings," Chloe explained. "When you're competitive, you're trying to beat someone. It's a bad thing."

For Chloe, like many of her girlfriends, competing doesn't feel like it's just about trying to do your best. It's about trying to do something better than someone else, in a hurtful and not nice way. Competition is conveyed to many young girls as the way that you challenge someone publicly, even if you might lose. Competing means sweaty hands, butterflies in your stomach (not the good kind), and sometimes tears. Competing is a bad word.

Nearly every woman I know can think of a time when you were confident but reluctant to turn that inner strength into outward action and therefore missed a chance to make that moment a defining one, personally or professionally. When you were faced with a new challenge, but self-doubt set in and you were not sure what to do next. When moving forwards required not just personal conviction but audacious action. We've all been there, likely more than once. Our girls have those moments, too.

For Chloe, it was when her dad made her enter the Year 6 geography bee.

For Sophia, now in Year 9, it was when she didn't make the swimming team in in her first years of primary school. Her parents, competitive athletes in college, had encouraged her to find a sport she'd enjoy and hopefully thrive in. Sophia loved swimming with her grandfather during the summer, so they thought the pool would be where she'd find athletic inspiration. Sophia worked all summer to master her strokes, hoping to become part of the swimming club's youth team. Her mum was by her side throughout, motivating her in part with reminders that practices were special time away from her younger brother. She was thrilled when she finally earned a spot on the roster in Year 4. Then the swimming meets started and she came in last. Every time. "Not just last," admitted her mum, "but last last. Last by an entire length of the pool." Sophia wondered whether competing was worth it.

For Grace, the moment was on my couch after receiving gut-wrenching "We regret to inform you..." letters from not just one or two but five college admissions offices. She was resilient enough to keep showing up to class, talk about what was on her mind, and even continue congratulating friends for the good news they'd received from universities. But she wasn't sure what to do next. Or how she could throw herself back into the next phase of the college application process, which meant re-engaging with two universities that had wait-listed her. Grace couldn't imagine diving back into the competition. The idea wasn't just daunting. It was unbearable.

Where these girls' stories differ from those of many peers who haven't been prepared and supported in the same way lies in what happens when faced with those "what next?" moments and how they handle the next hour, day, or chapter of both the school year and life. It's easy to imagine traits like confidence and resilience coming to our girls' aid in these moments—and there is a lot of contemporary research to support the idea that these skills help girls own their potential, adapt to challenges, and persist through adversity. But even as we acknowledge the importance of resilience and confidence, especially for our girls, we undervalue the role that a competitive spirit plays. We need to teach our girls to embrace competition and develop critical skills that will help them compete effectively, as kids and adults. Getting comfortable with healthy competition will help girls face whatever challenge comes their way—especially when we define challenge not as a conflict against an individual or even a team, but as a struggle against a system or way of being. Sometimes even a struggle against gender bias and discrimination.

Why introduce the contentious idea of competitiveness into the mix? In the context of what girls need to succeed, why consider how to nurture a young women's competitive spirit?

Being able to compete effectively is an asset not just in sports but also in many other aspects of life. Yet it's an advantage that girls too often hand over to boys, to their detriment. Research shows that women in general respond less favourably to competition than men. Statistics demonstrate that we are less eager to compete, despite the many twenty-first-century initiatives designed to even the playing field for women so that we might more readily succeed when we take part in whatever game, literal or metaphorical, is under way. Experiments suggest that we perform worse than men in competitive arenas, even when we have the skills to excel at whatever task is at hand. So fewer women enter and win any given contest—whether it's a race or a match of some sort, the chance to compete for a job or promotion, or just the opportunity to speak aloud. Ultimately that means women realize fewer benefits from efforts to create an even playing field because we opt out of competition and instead pursue other, more circuitous paths towards advancement.

A healthy competitive spirit is the edge girls need to be audacious women. Which is why one of the best things we can do for our young girls is help them develop the healthy competitive spirit that seems to come so easily to boys. Doing so means nurturing in our daughters the sense of excitement about competition that helps you push yourself to win a match or game, and that doesn't equate doing so with a value judgement about another person. In the process, we'll give our girls the skills they need to compete in the real-world situations they'll face later in life.

I was always comfortable being competitive on a basketball court or sports field, but I didn't realize the true real-world value of a competitive spirit until I was in the Navy. When I faced the sort of challenges that required not just a little more confidence, a little more perseverance, and a little more bravery but also the ability to act on those feelings. As a naval officer, I wanted that proverbial seat at the table but needed a slightly more strategic set of skills and the assertive attitude to do so effectively. I needed to embrace the healthy competitive spirit that my peers, most of whom were men, tapped into with ease and bravado.

One afternoon, a few weeks into the final, most rigorous phase of flight school training, I slunk back from the flight line where we'd parked the jet, keeping my eyes down on the tarmac and trying to avoid seeing anyone as I headed to the squadron ready room. I had floundered through an extended mock dog-fight in my T-2 Buckeye jet, throwing up throughout while simultaneously trying to master air-to-air combat manoeuvres. I'd never felt more miserable, physically and mentally.

Wanting some time and space to catch my breath—and to surreptitiously throw away the three full puke bags that were stuffed in a pocket of my flight suit—I sneaked off to the second-floor ladies' room. Leaning against a cracked bathroom counter, I hoped to quiet the cramped muscles in my legs and shoulders and pat dry the flight suit that clung to my back and neck, damp with sweat from flying a two-hour mission in the middle of a summer heat wave.

As I tried in vain to stop crying before my eyes became red and puffy, I heard the door of a nearby bathroom stall swing open. I had company in what I'd hoped would be a private ladies' room breakdown. I pretended to fastidiously wash my hands, but when I sneaked a look to my right, my stomach dropped further, if that was possible.

Standing tall in her specially embroidered "shit hot" flight suit was Lieutenant Shannon, the only female instructor pilot in my squadron. And the only female F/A-18 Hornet pilot I'd met. The combination of her standoffish demeanour, combat stories, and long blond hair meant that she had a small group of follow-ers and fans – including me – who silently kept tabs on her and cheered for her every achievement. We were a handful of women who hoped to graduate from flight school and follow in her foot-steps, straight into the cockpit of a fighter jet.

What Girls Need

I grabbed a fistful of stiff paper towels to blot my tearstained face. Maybe she wouldn't notice me. Or maybe she would notice me and would give me a sisterly pep talk. I'm not sure which I wanted more.

A few seconds passed as Lieutenant Shannon finished rinsing her hands and began tightening the bun in her hair to comply with the Navy's grooming standards for women.

Then without acknowledging me or even glancing in my direction, she said to the bathroom mirror, "Whatever you do, don't let them see you cry. Put on your game face."

It was time to throw myself back into the competition.

Why does that moment in the ladies' room still come to mind when I'm faced with what feels like an insurmountable challenge? Why did I remember Lieutenant Shannon's voice when I talked with Chloe about how she felt when she was at her geography bee, worried about the contest that was unfolding around her? Why does the phrase "put on your game face" loom large in my mind when I hear Sophia talk about the swimming team or Grace speak about navigating the college process?

It's for the same reason that, when Baldwin's primary school director talks about the most critical lessons we teach our girls, she pauses before divulging one particular lesson as if to ensure no one will overhear her sharing a dirty secret. And then she explains how important it is to help our youngest students learn how to compete—not just how to manage competition but how to embrace it, too.

"If you set it up right, if you do it right, learning to compete helps them decide which of their internal goals matter most, practise dealing with disappointment and defeat, and figure out how to play real-world games," she tells me. "Why wouldn't we want to help with that?"

Even as we have focused on raising our girls to be confident, teaching them to be resilient, and nurturing them to be brave, we've largely overlooked one of the most critical foundational skills necessary to turn those lessons into bold action. We've forgotten to teach them how to enjoy and thrive in competition.

▌ Wait... Competition Is Good for Kids?

First, let's dispel the myth that competition in and of itself is bad—and that competitiveness must be discouraged in children at all costs.

For centuries, scholars have passionately debated the influence of competition in all its forms. Any description of Darwin's theory of evolution, Adam Smith's writings on economics, or Sun Tzu's strategies for warfare will no doubt include mention of what's good—and bad—about competition in nature, in institutions, and for society. Even the Roman poet Ovid voiced his opinion on the matter, noting in *The Art of Love* that "A horse never runs so fast as when he has other horses to catch up and outpace."

In the late nineteenth century, social scientists like Norman Triplett shifted our attention to the role of competition in everyday life. Born on an Illinois farm in 1861, Triplett was known to his friends as an athletic young man, a science teacher, and the first American to win a gold medal for running the 100-yard dash in under ten seconds. In modern history books, he's also credited with conducting the first laboratory experiment in the field of social psychology. Triplett's love of cycling inspired him to study results from the 1897 League of American Wheelmen races, a series of contests sponsored by and for some of the country's most fanatical cyclists. He had noticed that cyclists were recording faster race times when riding against one another as opposed to just against a clock. Nearly five seconds per mile faster.

So Triplett decided to figure out whether the mere presence of another person in a race would improve performance. Whether having another participant by a rider's side arouses a competitive instinct, providing "the means of releasing or freeing nervous energy for him that he cannot of himself release." No doubt picturing his own experience on a bicycle, Triplett theorized that competition provides the inspiration we all need to make a greater effort and perform better overall.

Blending his schoolteaching experience with his new studies, he set up a laboratory experiment to test this theory. Triplett asked forty children aged ten to twelve years old to use a fishing reel contraption to move a flag sixteen metres as fast as possible—first alone, and then again while racing a second child. He took extensive notes while watching the races, even commenting how a few kids with an "exceedingly nervous temperament" performed compared with their peers and noting that the two children who were left-handed were slower because he'd built the machine to be used with your right hand.

What remains most relevant to this day was Triplett's analysis showing that competing against another person did materially impact most kids' performance. Some children made a small improvement in their race time. Others, about 25 per cent, found the competitive nature of the race overstimulating and slowed slightly. But twenty children—50 per cent of the participants—got significantly better, speeding up by a few seconds on each race. Triplett concluded that "the desire to beat, if it did nothing else, brought them to a sense of what was possible." In other words, whether you win or lose, competition helps you improve.

Over the next century, researchers tried to build on Triplett's work or prove him wrong, looking at various aspects of a competition to figure out what about competitive systems was beneficial or detrimental, to individuals and groups. As Po Bronson and Ashley Merryman describe in their book *Top Dog: The Science of Winning and Losing*, which reviews hundreds of studies from neuroscience, psychology, athletics, finance, education, and more, most people improve when competing. Yes, competition can bring out the worst in people in certain situations; extreme forms of "maladaptive competitiveness" include overly aggressive behaviour, unsportsmanlike conduct, and even cheating to win. But by and large, a well-run tournament, contest, or other form of competition motivates us to try harder, inspires us to overcome fears and take risks, and improves our performance on individual tasks.

Take, for example, the results when competitive games were

used to help middle school students improve their arithmetic skills. One study conducted a few years ago by researchers from New York University compared competition with collaboration to determine what made a game "good" for learners, where good outcomes included improved fluency in the subject matter, higher levels of student motivation, and greater engagement and interest in the learning process. Fifty-eight boys and girls in a technology-themed after-school programme for middle school children were randomly assigned to play Factor Reactor, an educational computer game that asks players to add, subtract, multiply, and divide numbers to solve an increasingly difficult set of maths problems. While playing, they practised the basic arithmetic skills that are critical for and often lacking in students that age. Picture pre-algebra class meets flash cards meets an Xbox game.

The key for this experiment was that some kids played on their own with instructions to "get the best score you can", others played against a second player in class and were told to "compete against each other for the better score", and some were given a partner and asked to "work together to get the best score". Analysis of the results measured how the students performed (the number of problems they answered correctly), how much they improved along the way (the progression to harder levels of the game over time), whether they achieved long-term learning goals (improved performance on an arithmetic test after playing the game for about twenty minutes), and so forth.

As with Triplett's findings, competition made a positive difference. The kids who played against a peer performed much better, statistically speaking, than those playing either on their own or with a friend. While both the competitive and collaborative approach to the game improved kids' motivation to learn and excitement for solving arithmetic problems, pure skills acquisition was most improved when it was framed as a fun but competitive game.

Or consider research by Harvard Business School's Daniel Gross, who tested how competition influences people's creativity and originality. He collected data from 122 online logo contests, in which firms solicited custom artwork from freelance designers who hoped to win the recognition—and cash prize—given to the winning entry. About thirty-five "players" participated in each contest, during which they were given a brief description of the business and audience for which the logo would be used and were provided private real-time feedback on their submissions along the way. Players could update or resubmit designs as often as they wanted until the competition ended and a winning design was selected. Over the course of a few weeks, about a hundred individual logo designs were submitted for each contest.

What unfolded was an interactive process during which designers would submit logos, receive feedback from the business involved, and iterate their work over multiple days in hopes of winning the design contest and a few hundred dollars. In one example, a designer submitted three images to help rebrand an Israeli rockabilly band called the MollyCoddles who wanted to update their logo. Even to a casual observer, two of the artist's designs appeared quite different—one used a picture of an Elvis-esque bandleader strumming a guitar; the other had a rock-and-roll baby crooning into a mike, complete with a skull tattoo on the infant's arm. Meanwhile, the third submission just tweaked the font and colouring of a previously submitted design. It appeared that the artist had lost his motivation that round, put in less effort, and settled for something far less creative. The key was to determine how the competitive aspect of the contest influenced this designer.

Not trusting casual observations to study this question, Gross developed a computer algorithm that compared how similar or different contestants' designs were to previous submissions—how "original" each image was—and correlated these findings with how highly they were rated by the reviewing sponsors, who ultimately judged the designs and picked winners. After analyzing more than 11,750 logo submissions, Gross discovered that the competitive pressure of a contest format motivated designers to produce more original designs. In fact, while heavy competition eventually pushed participants to stop investing in the contest, he concluded that some competition is necessary for even the highest performers to produce their most creative, original work. Absent that motivation, the participating artists tended to simply tweak earlier work rather than breaking through into untested territory.

Other researchers have looked at how competition can improve risk-taking, how competition motivates groups, and more—demonstrating that competition, when framed correctly and introduced appropriately, provides concrete benefits for adults and children. In other words, it's time to rethink our aversion to competition in all its forms. Especially for our girls.

▌ Is Competitiveness Okay, Too?

Social science research aside, parents and teachers nevertheless remain concerned about what happens when competition is introduced at school or when adults teach children to compete in other places. Won't our kids become competitive? Is that okay? Do our kids really need to know how to compete? And if they do need to compete, must they behave competitively?

Hopefully, this is when you're rolling your eyes and admitting that yes, competition is part of your everyday life as an adult. You're thinking about the 5K race you ran recently or last week's game of pickup basketball or fantasy football. Maybe you're remembering applying for graduate school or thinking about watching elections unfold in the news and noting the competitive aspect of public debates.

But what about when you tried to buy your first home or made plans to invest any money you set aside from your paycheque? Or when you were applying for your first job, and later going for that promotion? How about when you wanted to audition for the local community play or throw your hat in the ring to lead your congregation or become president of the school parents' association? All of these everyday acts and many more require a healthy level of competitiveness—the ability to opt into a contest, strive to be your best, open yourself up to critique as you're judged against peers, and ultimately win or lose gracefully.

With these examples in mind, we all might readily accept that competition is necessary in life and that real-world "success" is often paired with a competitive nature. But you still might be surprised to realize just how important a healthy competitive spirit is and how critical this trait, and the skills that come with it, is to those who thrive in business, entrepreneurship, academia, and other fields that our girls want to enter when they grow up.

In business, over 90 per cent of the executives leading Fortune 500 companies—those C-suite professionals whom we hold up as exemplars of success in the corporate world—were competitive athletes when they were young. This holds true for the women at the top, too. When Ernst & Young surveyed 821 senior managers and executives on their perspective about sports, approximately 90 per cent of the women sampled said they played competitive sports in primary, middle, or secondary school. That number went up to an astonishing 94 per cent among women in the most senior, C-suite positions, most of whom were competitive athletes in college, too.

Did you know that Meg Whitman, the former CEO of Hewlett-Packard, played squash and lacrosse as a child and continued in both sports at Princeton? Or that as a teenager, Christine Lagarde, the first woman to become finance minister of a major industrial country and who is now the president of the European Central Bank, was on the French national synchronized swimming team? Or that Michelle Brooke-Marciniak, cofounder of SHEEX, a start-up that produces high-performance bedding, was an All-American collegiate athlete and professional basketball player who played point guard in the WNBA?

What's more, these women believe that the lessons they learned as athletes were critical to their personal and professional

Cultivate Her Competitive Spirit

achievement later in life. When asked about the factors that help women most, 74 per cent of female executives said that a background in sports can help accelerate a woman's career.

Brooke-Marciniak credits her time as a basketball player with the competitive drive that helped her succeed, explaining how it created an internal motivation that she used to push herself on a daily basis. "I always had to rewind the film [to study her performance after a game] twenty times, touch every line while running sprints, and hit one extra shot before I left the gym. I don't know if that's obsessive, but that's the drive that I have." Other female corporate leaders note that learning to compete translated into a toughness that helped them hold their own in non-athletic contexts. Particularly in male-dominated environments. Laura Gentile, a senior vice president at ESPN and one of *Forbes*'s Most Powerful Women in Sports, credits her time as a competitive field hockey player for giving her this edge later in life. "I have held my own with boys and men on the athletic field for a long time... I think I just came in with a toughness and I've certainly developed thicker skin that just helps you keep going."

It wasn't the level of sport the women played but the mere fact that they played at all that mattered.

The need to be competitive is also critical for politics, where women remain significantly under-represented among elected officials. Despite recent efforts to shift that dynamic, including formal programmes designed to encourage more women to run for public office, only about 24 per cent of the members of our federal legislature are female and 10 per cent of state governorships. Research shows that the highly competitive nature of political campaigns still has a negative influence on whether potential female candidates throw their hat into the ring. One recent study surveyed over 1,500 women and men, with both conservative and liberal leanings, to test their interest in getting elected. It showed that women's interest in running for office dropped from 20 per cent to 5 per cent when the election process was described as highly competitive. Meanwhile, 30 per cent of men said they wanted to learn more about running either way. The competitiveness needed to gain and hold political positions has "a strong negative effect on women's interest in political office, but not on men's interest."

Competition doesn't impact men's choices in the same detrimental way. In fact, a willingness to compete often gives men the upper hand even as it puts women at a disadvantage. Beyond politics and the corporate world, this gender disparity also emerges in academia, in Silicon Valley, and even in the investment world, where women's approach to financial planning and managing financial assets has been the subject of scrutiny.

In contrast, women with a healthy competitive spirit often thrive in even the most high-stakes situations. For Adrienne Harris, former chief business development officer at a Silicon Valley financial services start-up and prior to that a White House senior advisor, knowing how to compete naturally and effectively helped her succeed in every male-dominated environment she's found herself in. "I often think about my professional life like a game. It helps me take things less personally, and then I engage my competitiveness when it's most helpful," she told me.

"It's not about not 'liking' someone or wanting to 'beat'

someone," Adrienne continued. "It's about understanding the rules of the game so you can be and do your best. I learned the rules in the White House, at my old law firm, and in Silicon Valley. And then I was able to play the game effectively."

When we started talking about her status as a black woman in these arenas, she added, "I hadn't thought about it as competitiveness, but in retrospect, that's part of what helps me raise my hand in meetings, speak up when I have an opinion, and more generally, swing for the fences, professionally speaking. Especially when I'm the only one in the room who looks like me."

She paused, and then added almost as an afterthought, "Actually, it's not just about playing effectively. I like playing to win, too."

In other words, we can't ignore the fact that a healthy competitive spirit opens up an area of our personalities that we need, and that our kids also need, to succeed. Kids who are comfortable competing and embrace sportsmanlike behaviour will be able to, as adults, opt into the normal contests of life, push themselves to excellence, and be comfortable with both winning and losing. We can't overlook the fact that girls need to know how to play the game, too—and that making sure they do might take special support and encouragement from the adults in their lives. This idea becomes particularly critical when you consider what competing "like a girl" often looks like and see all the behavioural norms that we have been conditioned to accept when we watch our daughters in competitive arenas. If we see those moments with fresh eyes, our girls appear to be at a disadvantage. At least if we let these ideas perpetuate themselves.

▌ Is Competing "Like a Girl" a Real Thing?

As concerns have grown about gender inequities in and out of the workplace, more and more attention has been spent considering why, even as women appear to be statistically closing the gap in educational settings, women still lag behind men when it comes to pay and opportunities for advancement. Even though women in the United States earn more undergraduate and graduate degrees than men (60 per cent to 57 per cent, respectively), they are under-represented across senior levels of every sector. Fewer than 15 per cent of corporate executives are women, and women hold fewer than 20 per cent of corporate board seats. Only 20 per cent of partners in law firms are women, even though women represent about half of the associates entering the legal profession. And so on.

Women are graduating at higher rates and pursuing jobs in historically male-dominated sectors, but it appears that they are ultimately opting out of competitive workplaces and succeeding less often in professional competitions. Social norms and family-centred decisions are likely at play, but researchers also wonder whether these outcomes reflect the fact that women simply don't like to compete as much as men do. That natural gender differences are at play, halting many women's forward professional progress.

But what if it's not nature causing this effect? What if instead social norms, education, and upbringing are dampening girls' competitive spirit and thus inhibiting their career and personal success? What if nurture, not nature, is the culprit?

With these questions in mind, a team of researchers from the

Cultivate Her Competitive Spirit

University of Chicago and Columbia University set out to study how culture influences girls' inclination to compete. They decided to peel back the layers from one of the most entrenched aspects of modern Western society by comparing people's competitiveness in matriarchal versus patriarchal systems. The team spent time with the Masai tribe of Tanzania, a strongly patriarchal society in which men control wealth, status, and decision-making, and the Khasi tribe of India, a matrilineal society in which women are the heads of their households and social and monetary influence is passed down through a mother's youngest daughter. The hope was to examine age-old questions about the effect of nature versus nurture, through the lens of competitiveness.

Over the course of a few days with each tribe, groups of men and women were asked to perform a simple task—throwing a ball into a bucket from a distance of about three metres—with the option to be paid a small financial reward for each successful toss or, if they opt into a contest framework from the start, to be paid three times that amount for outperforming a peer. A simple way to test the question "Does competition motivate women and men equally?"

In other words, is there such a thing as competing "like a girl"? Is there truth behind the commonly held idea that our daughters compete differently, maybe because we assume they are more sensitive, less interested in winning, or exhibit other behaviours often expected of young girls?

The results of this experiment were staggering. In the Masai community, which promotes Western-style gender norms, men were shown to be more competitive than women. But in the matriarchal Khasi tribe, where one man even complained that he and his friends were "sick of playing the roles of breeding bulls and babysitters", women were more competitive than men: 54 per cent of women chose to compete, whereas only 39 per cent of men opted into the competitive and possibly more rewarding framework. In fact, Khasi women were slightly more competitive than men in the Masai tribe (54 per cent versus 50 per cent). As it turns out, women and men do compete differently, but it's because they've been conditioned that way.

It's natural for researchers and parents alike to ask how and when social conditioning impacts children's competitive nature. Do adults and kids differ in these contexts? So a team of researchers ventured back to the aforementioned Khasi tribe and sought out the Meghalaya tribe, a nearby indigenous group in northeast India who are evolutionarily similar to the Khasi in nearly every respect, except that the Meghalaya have a male-dominated social structure like we do in the West.

The same "toss a tennis ball into a bucket" test was performed, this time with over three hundred girls and boys, ages seven to fifteen. Again, the results were striking. Across both tribes, the youngest kids—those up to age twelve—were remarkably similar in their desire and willingness to compete. Both the girls and boys opted for the more competitive version of the game, where they won bigger prizes if they beat an opponent, about half the time. There was no difference across gender or culture when it came to children's competitive spirit.

But, around puberty, things started to change. In the patriarchal Meghalaya tribe, girls became less competitive after age thirteen, even as the boys became more competitive. In the matriarchal Khasi tribe, the outcome was exactly the opposite. When they became teenagers, the girls became more competitive and the boys started to shy away from competition.

You're no doubt wondering whether lessons from indigenous ethnic groups halfway around the world apply to raising children in our fast-paced twenty-first-century society. Researchers had the same concerns, so they turned to communities in Sweden, Austria, Israel, and Armenia to test these theories about the factors that influence kids' competitive nature. The studies re-affirmed the fact that culture matters—a lot.

For example, consider the work of Alison Booth and Patrick Nolen, two economists affiliated with the influential IZA Institute of Labor Economics who tested how girls and boys from four different schools in Essex, England, reacted to competition. The key differentiator for the children involved was in how they were nurtured—in other words, what environment supported and shaped them. Half of the schools involved were co-educational schools, while half were all-girls and all-boys schools. Two hundred and sixty boys and girls, most of whom were just under fifteen years old, were asked to solve a series of mazes in five minutes' time. After two rounds, they were given the option of receiving about fifty pence per maze solved correctly or four times that amount per maze for solving more mazes than peers in their group.

The results echoed those seen in northeast India. Girls from an all-girls school—the modern equivalent of the matriarchal Khasi community—chose to enter the contest just as much as boys from either a co-educational or single-sex school. They wanted to compete just like the boys did. Meanwhile, girls from co-educational schools in this experiment opted into the tournament less often than girls from single-sex schools, and less than boys from either school. The researchers concluded that a girl's environment plays a critical role in whether she chooses to compete, suggesting that gender differences we observe in competitive arenas reflect social learning. In other words, when it comes to competition, girls can be raised to enthusiastically embrace their competitive instincts, even in Western or patriarchal society.

What's more, if we return to Triplett's study from the turn of the twentieth century, with those forty kids and the fishing reel contest, we see the positive influence of girls' competitive natures. If we analyze his data to consider how girls were impacted by head-to-head competition, we find that the girls responded, on the whole, much better than the boys. A much higher percentage of girls than boys responded favourably to the competitive scenario (62 per cent versus 29 per cent). Moreover, the girls saw greater improvements in their race times when the experiment was set up as a contest against a peer.

In other words, despite what we see in the real world right now, girls do like to compete. And they do compete effectively. But doing so depends on how a girl is raised and nurtured along the way.

▌ What's a Parent to Do?

When I tell parents and teachers about this research, they are generally aghast and sometimes a bit embarrassed.

Cultivate Her Competitive Spirit

After recovering from their surprise and more often than not clarifying which reward structure they'd choose if I paid them to throw a tennis ball into a bucket, most parents ask, "What should I do?" Like any adult caring for a young girl, they want to know how they can make sure their daughter isn't at a disadvantage. They want to ensure she's prepared to enter the world with the same healthy competitive spirit that, research and daily experience show, boys more naturally adopt and more effectively call upon, as kids and as adults, in so many aspects of life.

The good news is that how we nurture our girls when they're young makes a big difference. There are things we can do to help them grow into adult women who are not just resilient, confident, and brave but also know how to use those important traits to lean into competitive arenas and nab exciting opportunities when they have the chance—even when it requires going head-to-head with someone else. We must ensure that our girls don't confuse lessons about the need to be empathetic community members, who are kind to their classmates and good team players, with the message that acting on their healthy competitiveness—including by opting into contests, pushing yourself to excellence, and being prepared to win or lose—is a bad thing.

The key is to reframe how we think and talk about competition, to consciously model competitiveness for our girls, and to help our girls practise the basic skills needed to compete effectively. In the same way that we describe "good" and "bad" cholesterol, we must explain to our daughters that there is "good" and "bad" competitiveness, show them examples of healthy and effective female competitors, and find ways for them to embrace the constructive competitiveness that will be so essential when they're adults. These basic steps will give our girls the swagger and skills that they need to compete effectively and succeed no matter what comes next.

▌ The Impact of Our Words

First, let's start with the obvious. We as parents and teachers have to reframe our thinking about competition and competitiveness. It's not toxic. And it's certainly not just for boys. As both research and real-world experience show, a healthy appreciation for competition can motivate people to try harder, help them find resilience during difficult times, inspire them to be selfless teammates, and even improve their creativity. What's more, the ability to tap into your competitive spirit and opt into a contest is a fantastic skill for *all* children and young adults, but especially for girls and young women. We need to overhaul the way we think about competitiveness in general, and to come up with new techniques that encourage our girls to embrace competition. We should aim to transform competing "like a girl" from an insult into a compliment.

The need for this mindset shift was no more apparent than during my conversation with Chloe, when she was describing the evils of competitiveness—and then admitting that her little brother, Teddy, was super competitive, and that was okay.

"I don't think I'm competitive," she started, pausing to think about it a bit. "I try, but I'm not good at it. I don't play sports, so I don't think I've had many chances. And boys are definitely more competitive. They are always trying to beat someone and be the best. Teddy is like that."

"What about your girlfriends? What do you all think about competing?" I asked, curious if she had any impression of "good" versus "bad" competitiveness.

"Girls can be competitive. But we realize it's stupid, so we're, like, 'whatever,'" she continued. "And I don't want to be unkind to people ... I don't want to hurt people's feelings."

When her mum reminded her how excited she is to play and win during card games with her family, Chloe replied, "At home, I can be competitive, and it won't matter. I'm not going to be criticized for that."

"Good" competitiveness didn't exist in Chloe's twelve-year-old view. If she wasn't in the safe space of home and family, it was all bad. At least for her and her female classmates, even as the boys could take advantage of their competitive spirit.

A few feet away, Chloe's mum was astounded by her daughter's comments. "I'm horrified. I had no idea she felt this way," she shared in a moment of heartfelt candour. "I knew that the geography bee had been an issue, but I didn't realize it was because she was reluctant to compete against her friends or show how much she knew."

As our conversation continued, Chloe's mum reflected on how she and her husband talked about competition at home—or, more often, how they didn't.

"I'm competitive. I've always played sports. I was a competitive football player in college. Chloe knows that. I thought she would have naturally picked up on it being a good thing," Chloe's mum said.

What became clear as we continued talking was that while both of Chloe's parents had a healthy competitive spirit, they didn't talk about it explicitly with their daughter. They'd both been competitive athletes growing up, and as adults had competed for big jobs, participated in running and cycling races, and more. But they hadn't made it a point of casual but conscientious discussion with their kids—especially with their little girl, who had grown up opting out of contests instead of understanding that there was "good" competitiveness.

To help Chloe and her friends shift their thinking, we need to be mindful of how we respond to girls when they lean into their competitive spirit. We need to encourage their competitiveness, just as we do for boys, to normalize the idea that it's okay for our daughters to embrace their competitive natures and that girls shouldn't be embarrassed or ashamed of being "good" competitors.

One strategy by which your family can exalt a healthy competitive spirit is to celebrate your own wins, bringing family role models front and centre for your girls. In Chloe's case, her mum lamented that she hadn't been more open with her kids when she was competing for a new job, so that she and her husband could explain what it was like to throw your hat into the ring against other people and push yourself to be your best, no matter the outcome. The idea is to help our daughters see that they can lift themselves up and put themselves forward for a job or another exciting opportunity without diminishing others. That competition is not about undercutting other people but instead is an important aspect of self-advocacy.

"I wish I'd talked more about how I was putting myself up for this promotion and what it felt like to compete with others along the way," said Chloe's mum, a primary school administrator who had recently stepped into a new, more senior role.

"I wish that when I got the new job, my husband and I had more openly celebrated it as the big win that it was." Perhaps, then, Chloe would see that it was okay for her to be competitive, too. Like her mum.

In addition to establishing role models at home, we should talk about the women our girls see on social media, on TV, or in the news whose competitiveness is a clear asset. This includes pointing out athletes, politicians, and entrepreneurs who dig into their competitive spirit to overcome failure, face down gender bias, and find success. When you next see a woman win (or lose) a major contest, athletic event, or competition, point it out to your daughter. Find a video online of the final round of the contest, and watch it with her. Help her visualize what it means to be a competitive woman.

When Serena Williams lost the 2018 U.S. Open, we did just that at my school. One of Baldwin's high school clubs watched different videos of Williams in the tournament, as a teacher led a group discussion about her performance on and off the court. They also talked about Naomi Osaka, the twenty-year-old rising tennis star who beat Williams in the final round. In many ways, it didn't matter where the conversation led. It just mattered that the girls were given powerful images of female competitors and that they saw adults whom they respect taking women's competitiveness seriously. For a few minutes, competing "like a girl" was a strength, not a weakness.

In Practice, It Means Practice

It's also critical to help girls practise the skills that over time make the act of competing easier and more natural, so they get used to being effective, healthy competitors. Girls who rehearse and polish their competitive skill set will find that it becomes routine to opt into a contest, push yourself to excellence, embrace the opportunity to show off your talents, and grow used to the discomfort and uncertainty that comes before and during competition. They will also learn important lessons about how to be a good sport after either a win or a loss and will grow more comfortable with the complicated (and sometimes even negative) feelings that can accompany both winning and losing. Along the way, our girls will realize that those "bad" feelings you have during competition—the killer instinct, the desire to defeat another, the drive to outthink your opponent—aren't the same as being mean. And really aren't bad at all. Practice helps our girls see that a healthy competitive spirit is not in tension with their desire to be team-oriented and kind or to demonstrate empathy, nor does it equate with hurting others even when there are winners and losers.

The first step to cultivating practice is to find moments for your daughter to join a competition and then encourage her to participate—whether it's a sport, a board game, a spelling bee, or even the chance to try out for the school play. The type of contest doesn't matter. Nor does the outcome of whatever tournament she enters. The simple reality of choosing to compete and then knowing you'll give it your all is what's key.

When your child is young, from reception to Year 4, practising competition can be as easy as playing Old Maid, Connect Four, Sorry!, or other games with your daughter. Even the most basic childhood games typically have a tournament aspect to them, because game designers realize that's what makes games fun and engaging. So resist the inclination that some parents have lately to shun such games in the name of wiping out "bad" competitiveness from family fun. Instead, actively find time to play these games with your girls, and even as you keep it light-hearted, remind them that it's good to play your best, okay to want to win, and necessary to be gracious when you lose—all basic aspects of being a good competitor.

Also remember that practising competition isn't about letting your daughter win. From an early age, children should experience both winning and losing so that they build resilience in the face of defeat, learn to be kind and generous when they win, and also don't mistakenly think that being a winner means never losing.

Mario, a father of two girls at my school who freely admits that he's competitive by nature, shared his personal strategy for teaching these lessons. The first few times he plays a new board game with his Year 4 daughter, he talks her through his moves. He uses early rounds to explain the strategy behind the game so she can learn to compete on her own. Then once she builds up her comfort level, he slowly ups the competition. Over time, Mario realized that modeling competitiveness this way helped teach his eight-year-old to play to win, to be a good sport, and to be resilient in the face of setbacks. He somewhat sheepishly admits it makes it more fun for him, too. I understand that their last heated game of Connect Four ended in a draw.

When your child reaches Year 4 or so, cultivating a competitive spirit means actively embracing more formal competitions outside the home by tapping into whatever activity or subject matter your daughter finds most exciting. For example, for the girl who loves to read and write, check out your local library or bookshop to see what contests might be available. Our neighbourhood local library hosts a junior author contest every year, soliciting poetry, fiction, and non-fiction entries from Year 2 to Year 7 pupils. The chance to gain an audience for their work provides a great way for girls in our community to build a healthy competitive spirit, off the playing field. For those girls who like science and technology, check out the Technology Student Association (TSA), a nationwide organization that runs contests on technology, design, software development, and more for over 250,000 middle and secondary school students. It's an ideal opportunity for girls to practise the ins and outs of navigating a competitive arena. In the UK, look at TeenTech Innovations Sessions, which offer students, aged eleven to eighteen, insight into tech organizations and the opportunites that lie within them.

Yes, each child's work is subjectively assessed in these contests. Yes, there are first-, second-, and third-place prizes. But striving to earn a prize also presents an opportunity for our girls to take pride in their work, whether they receive an award or not.

Cultivate Her Competitive Spirit

And it helps them learn how to handle disappointment if they don't win. For girls, it's also an easy chance to have them practise the art and science of opting into a tournament setting and embracing healthy levels of competitiveness.

Also consider ways to encourage your daughter to run for elected positions at her school—whether it's class president, club head, or a leadership role for her area Girl Scouts or similar organization. These are moments when our girls need to actively compete to get the role, not just picture themselves leading the room. Listen for when your daughter mentions something that interests her, then see if there is a way she can put herself forward for more responsibility. In this way she can practise turning confidence into self-advocacy and voice, while also learning to recognize how and when to throw her hat into the ring for new opportunities. She will build critical "muscle memory" that will tell her, when she's older, to go for it when given the chance.

Sports Matter for Non-athletes, Too

Organized sports are also a fabulous option, especially as your girl enters middle school—whether or not your girl is a future Olympian; whether she might enjoy football or basketball, field hockey, or tennis. It doesn't matter what the sport is or even if it's a team sport, just so long as there is a contest involved that reinforces the practical skills required to effectively compete later in life. Even if they're not naturally athletic and even if they'll never get off the proverbial bench or win a big game, we parents should encourage our daughters to continue playing an organized sport through secondary school. Simultaneously, educators should find ways to include competitive sports in the daily schedule.

Studies show that playing competitive sports has a lasting positive impact and that girls who play team sports have more self-confidence and, despite the competitive nature of play, more readily learn important attributes of teamwork and sportsmanship. Student athletes are shown to perform better academically, too. What's more, the competitive spirit that girls learn by playing sports stays with them long after secondary school ends and has been correlated to high degrees of workplace success later in life.

This is one reason why continued gender disparity in sports should worry parents and educators. For our purposes, we should consider how this disparity feeds into cultural taboos that women carry about what it means to be nice and how it reinforces the stigmatization of girls' competitive instinct. There is ample reason to be concerned, especially since this form of gender disparity remains so widespread, even among school-aged children. According to the Women's Sports Foundation, by age fourteen, girls stop playing competitive sports twice as often as boys. This worrying trend continues into secondary school, where the attrition rates for girls in sports between Year 9 and the end of secondary school are two to three times higher than for boys. As a result, by age seventeen, over 50 per cent of teenage girls drop out of sports.

Which is where Sophia's swimming story comes in. And why I loved hearing that Sophia's parents didn't give up on their daughter playing sports, even after her disappointing season on the swimming team. Even after she told them: "This is exhausting. I don't want to do it anymore."

Sophia's mum, Patricia, explained, "We let it go and found other ways to keep her active, like biking on the weekend. But we're a family of athletes, so had a plan in mind for when Sophia got to Year 7. That would be when we'd have her try other sports, to see what team she'd join."

Her mum and dad didn't let it slide. They urged her back into the competitive arena, helping her explore a few different sports when she started middle school. Yes, she preferred singing and performing onstage at the local community theatre. But they also wanted her to have at least one sport to call her own. "We told her how important it was to play sports, even if you don't become an Olympic athlete."

After trying a few different teams, Sophia joined the school volleyball team. She played junior level the first year. The second, too. This year, in Year 9, she made the middle school A-team. "She's not the strongest," said her mum, "but she is so proud."

She has also learned the power of her competitive spirit. She understands how to turn the natural confidence that she feels when she's singing onstage—something Sophia loves to do and comes to quite naturally—into the sort of bold action that will help her later in life, particularly when she's pushed out of her comfort zone. That's what sports have always been for her.

So when it came time for Sophia to write her Year 9 class speech—a rite of passage for all her classmates; each one takes turns presenting a speech in front of the entire middle school—she didn't choose to talk about the last musical she performed in or the trip her family took last summer. Sophia gave a speech about sports and athletics. In her words, a speech about her "non-existent athletic career."

In her speech, Sophia described how her family is athletic. That her younger brother is training with elite junior football teams, hoping to one day play at a professional level. And that she can count how many times she served the volleyball over the net her first two years on the team: "Two. Just two."

She told a story about those swimming meets when she was in Year 6 and competing with swimmers from Year 2 and 3. "I came dead last... Every race," she said, laughing at herself.

But Sophia also shared why sticking with a competitive sport had been so rewarding. And why it made such a difference. She finished with a quote that was her new source of inspiration: "Winning isn't everything, but wanting to win is."

For Sophia, competing helped her turn confidence and resilience into bold action. On and off the volleyball court.

How Does It All Fit Together?

The key is not practising until perfect or playing on a championship team. Nor is it increasing feelings of competition surrounding your daughter so that the drive to win drowns out other skills we're trying to teach, including how to collaborate with others and be a good team player.

But we must not ignore the disparity that's currently at play when our girls are not nurtured to compete. We must actively find them role models who embrace their competitive spirit. We can't allow girls to shy away from competition because of fear or discomfort, or because they're concerned that competitiveness is something best left to boys. Our daughters need to get used to playing the game and knowing how to play to win, even if losing is okay, too. So they develop the skills that they need to compete effectively later in life, when "good" competitiveness becomes a much-needed asset.

Which is also why it's so important to consider how we as adults respond when fear, anxiety, or social pressures push our girls away from embracing competitions. For example, what happens when your daughter is too nervous to run for president of a school club or laments the fact that she's not athletic enough to play on the football team?

Before answering as the parent you are today, to the big kid you have in these circumstances, think back to what your response was when your daughter was fearful of riding the bus when she started primary school or uncomfortable sleeping at a friend's house the first time. Or how you—or perhaps think of a friend here—responded when your son didn't like the first or second sports team he tried? When I talk to parents about these ordinary instances of navigating childhood fears, I hear about all the creative ways they find small wins. Because we all know, for example, how important it is to master the basic skills of independently riding the bus or staying away from home for a night, we find ways to help our kids make progress towards these goals. Because for societal reasons we're less likely to let boys opt out of playing sports, I also hear from parents how they empower their sons to try a third, fourth, or even fifth sport until one sticks. Indeed, one family recently told me, with a mix of humour and exhaustion, how they'd tried baseball, basketball, and football for their son; he hated them all, but they wouldn't let him not play a sport in secondary school. Finally he started swimming. "He's not very athletic and won't ever be the star of the team. But he's found his sport."

It's time we do the same for our girls. If we want our daughters to have all the skills they need to succeed as adults, we need to more openly embrace the importance of our girls being good competitors and then help them figure out how and when to consciously tap into their competitive spirit. So that Chloe turns her confidence into action—not just for the geography bee but when she grows up and a job or other exciting opportunity presents itself. So that Sophia knows that pushing yourself to play the game as best you can is critical—not just for athletic competitions but for life. So that Grace understands the power of her game face from a young age and turns her resilience into action—throwing herself back into any game that's under way.

This aspect of empowering our girls was on my mind as Grace and I talked through her demoralizing college news. We sat side by side on the sofa in my office, and I listened to Grace voice her discouragement and dismay. Despite good grades, her volunteer work at a local hospital, and a touching personal essay about how her Korean heritage influenced what she wanted to study in college, Grace was denied or wait-listed at nearly every college on her list. In her mind, she'd put everything she had into school for so many years, and it was all for nothing. She was happy for friends who had been accepted into their dream schools, but couldn't figure out how to move forwards with her own post-secondary plans.

About halfway through our conversation, the tone of her voice and the focus of our discussion shifted. She started to speculate about what happens now and what to do next. We started to talk about re-engaging in the application process. It was my chance to talk about opting back into the competition. "It sounds like the process isn't quite done," I prompted. "What comes next, and how can I help?"

Grace looked up from her lap, where she'd been scrunching a dirty tissue between her fingers. She shrugged, even as her sad eyes still shone bright behind clear plastic eyeglass frames.

One college was left in the running, a distant choice both figuratively and literally. It was a dream school and would require moving to Chicago, far from family and friends. So we talked about what it would take to make that option a reality. How to not just persevere but lean back into the competitive process that is college applications—and life—so she could play the game alongside her peers.

Which is when I explained to Grace the concept of putting on your game face. When confronting real-life challenges, I often rely on more than self-confidence or grit to move forwards. Even if I'm not playing a sport and there's no clearly defined winner or loser, my competitive spirit helps me lean into whatever test I'm facing, whether to overcome that stint in flight school when I threw up during every training mission or when I wanted to finish my doctoral dissertation on the aggressive schedule set by my advisor. In those moments and more, I remember Lieutenant Shannon's "put on your game face" advice, reframe the challenge in my mind's eye, and tap into my competitive nature. It empowers me to face any roadblock with a bit more swagger, a bit more determination, and the attitude I need to succeed.

Grace nodded while we talked. But it wasn't until a year later that I knew she'd not just understood the need to compete but had also learned how to be a good competitor. How to put on her game face and thrive in the real world.

Over the summer, Grace moved across the country and made her best effort to enjoy first year at the University of Chicago. But when she realized the school just wasn't the right fit, she didn't let the idea of competing in the admissions process again deter her. She didn't assume that it was enough to persevere in the face of a tough college situation. Instead, she turned the resilience she'd built into bold action and again opted back into the trials of the college application process. So she could be judged once more against her peers and perhaps be rejected again. She embraced the chance to reapply for another dream school and, a year later, got news that she'd start her second year at her top choice university.

Grace's big win isn't just the college of her choice. It's knowing that she has the skills to effectively compete, whatever comes her way. That's what will make her not just successful in spirit but audacious in action, too.

She learned that it's not just okay for girls to embrace their competitive spirit. It's essential.

Nurture Her Collaborative Problem-Solving Skills

The sky was pitch-black as our jet circled over the western Pacific, hundreds of miles from dry land. We were totally alone, except for the lumbering Air Force KC-135 tanker looming a quarter of a mile in front of us, from which we planned to onload 10,000 gallons of fuel to continue our mission. The neon-green glow from my night-vision goggles magnified the intensity of the small lights on the tanker's drogue—a basketlike device dangling at the end of a long hose unfurled from the back of the tanker—that would pump fuel into our jet. We were trying to dock with what looked like an alien mother ship.

Noodle, my pilot, swiftly slowed our jet to about 300 knots, or 350 miles per hour, until we hovered a stone's throw behind the refuelling tanker. He inched the nose of our jet closer and closer to the other plane, aiming to fit the fuel probe at the tip of our jet into the drogue, which bobbed and weaved in the night air. For the next five minutes, he painstakingly moved our plane back and forth, trying to firmly lock on the tanker so we could refuel.

K-8, the third aviator in our jet, was calmly calling out numbers on the internal intercom, checking our airspeed and the distance to the tanker in front of us to make sure the two planes didn't collide.

The radios were silent. No one from the KC-135 would interrupt right now, while we were in the midst of one of the more difficult portions of midair refuelling—indeed, in reality one of the more stressful parts of any naval aviation mission.

As the second navigator in the jet, I grew more nervous as the minutes ticked by. It felt like hours had passed, and I still hadn't heard our pilot's calming "fuel transfer under way" message chirp across the intercom. Firmly secured in my ejection seat, I glanced into the cockpit and pulled off my night-vision goggles to better read the fuel gauges. My pulse sped up. I tapped my knuckles against the indicator, hoping that suddenly I'd see a different number. As if my "smack your iPhone to get the screen to unstick" trick worked in a military jet at 30,000 feet, in the middle of the Pacific Ocean.

We were low on fuel, given how far we were from the carrier. Dangerously low, given that there was no land—and therefore no airports—nearby either.

If we couldn't refuel from the tanker, what would we do?

Nurture Her Collaborative Problem-Solving Skills

When I remember being aloft in that jet, short on fuel in the middle of the world's largest ocean, my shoulders still grow tense. The flight was seared into my mind over a decade ago and about 8,000 miles from where I now sit, sipping lukewarm coffee. But that night still comes back to me in a flash. I have to stop myself from unconsciously reaching down to check my trouser pockets for a puke bag and to ensure the ejection handle is within reach. Just in case.

In my current role, leading an all-girls school, I find the story now takes on a new meaning—and matters more than ever before. I spend my waking hours imagining the future that our students will face one day and ensuring that we build a programme to prepare them for what's to come. When I recall scary moments from my personal and professional life while I am with these young women, the work we are all doing as parents, teachers, and our girls' cheerleaders comes into sharp focus. And I see the importance of lessons learned many years ago, including on that night in the jet—lessons that I didn't register at the time, while I was too immersed in the moment to see the bigger picture. It's only now, with distance and the perspective gained in my work as an educator, that I'm able to fully recognize the advantages that proved most useful throughout my career. And I discover lessons about what traits and ways of being we need to nurture in our girls, now more than ever.

It wasn't just the ability to tackle thorny challenges or address crises, even in complete darkness while flying at high subsonic speeds, that gave me the edge I needed to succeed. Nor was my edge the sole by-product of problem-solving on my own, under duress, and in extreme situations. Rather, it was the combination of the two that mattered most. It was my ability to coordinate and communicate with other people, to effectively leverage the power of group think to take on the most intense and complicated problems, even in life-threatening situations.

Ultimately, my great advantage was learning that collaborative problem-solving can save the day ... or the night, as the case may be. This lesson becomes even more relevant when we realize that collaborative problem-solving comes naturally to our girls and can be their competitive advantage for years to come, if it's nurtured effectively.

A Critical Skill for Her Future

This is when you might feel a sarcastic comment bubble up, or at the very least, you're thinking about skipping the next few pages. I get it. "Collaborative problem-solving" sounds a tad trendy and a little too much like educator lingo. What does this mean in the real world, and what impact does collaborative problem-solving have on the daily decisions we make with our daughters in mind? Can something so broad and seemingly obvious yield parenting advice that's specific to raising girls?

But imagine what daily life will look like for our kids ten or twenty years from now. Information will be even more readily

Nurture Her Collaborative Problem-Solving Skills

available than it is today, as technology like our now-ubiquitous smartphones and the ever-present internet is replaced by faster, easier ways to gather and share data. Remembering specific facts will be less important than making connections between readily available pieces of information. Rote memorization and flash cards, which many of us no doubt remember from school, will become even more fully a thing of the past. Instead, parents and educators will need to—and should already—increasingly focus on *how* our kids use the information at their fingertips, *how* they use it in relation to one another, and *how* they coordinate and communicate, work with others, and adapt in the face of challenges and change.

Jaime Casap is Google's chief education evangelist, a fancy title for the person leading the tech giant's effort to help reform our education system and better prepare the next generation for success in the workforce. According to Casap, the future awaiting our kids means that we should consciously find ways for them to practise collaborating on real-world problems—creating educational environments where they are "working together to create a solution... working together to build on a solution ... So they explore [a] topic, they explain [a] topic, they present [a] topic and their potential solutions... It's a very collaborative model."

When researchers talk about this increased need for "more than just knowledge and skills", they mean giving people the ability to draw on and leverage both information and "psychosocial resources, including skills and attitudes" to succeed. It's why some dental schools have started shifting from lectures to active learning strategies, using a collaborative pedagogy to develop critical-thinking and problem-solving skills in their dental students—and to promote increased self-confidence in their students as well. And why some law schools in Australia now prioritize giving students real-world problems, then providing practice, time, and training to help students solve those problems, thus attempting to bridge the gap between university and the actual practice of law, which requires working in teams and collaboratively tackling cases.

It's also what Jasmine, a talkative Year 9 pupil who likes Indian dance class as much as she likes coding, means when she's asked to describe the most important lessons she's learned, at home and in middle school. Without even taking a breath, she launches excitedly into stories of what she's learned that will help her with "tough situations" when she's older. Gesticulating emphatically, the thirteen-year-old leans forward on the couch, eager to convince me that being a good problem-solver is key.

"I don't really think about it now, because I'm a kid. But when I'm older, when I'm an adult and more independent, I'll have more freedom to decide what to do," she says, pausing to brush aside her long brown hair and search for the right words. "You need to be good at making decisions, and really good at solving problems. Especially with other people. That's what happens in the real world."

M y earpiece crackled as K-8 keyed the jet's internal intercom. "Chopper, we're not taking on fuel," she said, using my call sign and also showing a hint of the nervous energy that

Nurture Her Collaborative Problem-Solving Skills

I'd already felt creep through our cockpit. "We'll try one more time, but I don't think it's going to happen." K-8 paused, letting her words sink in.

We were literally in the middle of the ocean, short on fuel, with no airfield or land in sight and the aircraft carrier too far away to be much help at the moment. What's more, we were three of the most junior aviators in the squadron. I'd launched and trapped—that is, taken off and landed from the aircraft carrier—just a few dozen times. K-8 and Noodle didn't have much more experience than I did. This mission was starting to feel like sending a middle school softball team to the World Series, without a chaperone.

Mustering her courage, K-8 said, "I'll work with Noodle to see if there's a problem with the refuelling probe we can fix in flight. But we should start working a backup plan." Her suggestion hung in the cockpit. There weren't many good backup options.

"I'll start running numbers on our bingo fuel and see if there's any nearby airfield we overlooked," I replied, keying my mic while simultaneously pulling from my flight suit pocket the laminated manual that had instructions for the hundred plus emergencies that could happen while flying.

Every aviator spends countless hours reviewing this book and its crisis scenarios—in flight school, in simulators, during training flights, and at home on the couch—with the haunting advice of our instructors in mind. We learn how to deal with "bingo fuel", which is naval aviation slang for the perilous situation when your jet is critically low on fuel; technically, it means that you should head to the nearest land-based airport you can find, to ensure a safe landing. Unless, like us that night, there was no land around. Our instructors also teach us that "emergency procedures are written in the blood of fellow aviators, who have lived—and died—in the situations the manual describes. Know them well, and hopefully you won't write a new procedure yourself." Both these lessons were front of mind that night in the jet.

With the pocket-sized book in one hand, a map in the other, and a notepad strapped to my thigh, I flipped through the systematically organized manual, quickly thumbing past emergencies like engine failure, electrical/hydraulic failure, and fire/ejection to the pages that helped calculate how far we could fly on the fuel remaining to land safely.

I silently hoped there was some miraculous place near enough to divert to for an emergency landing if we couldn't make it back to the ship. Even if it was just an open field. In an emergency, it was always better to touch down on land, if possible, rather than trying one of the most difficult feats in the world—landing on an aircraft carrier, in the dark of night on a stormy sea, with no extra fuel for a cushion if it took multiple attempts to catch the wire.

I checked and double-checked before keying the internal intercom again, then selected the setting that ensured our pilot, Noodle, couldn't hear me. It was important for him to stay focused on keeping our jet aloft and out of harm's way. K-8 and I would figure out what to do next.

"K-8, it's not looking good," I started, trying not to sound as anxious as I felt. "There's no divert airfield we can make from here. They're too far, and we don't have enough gas. We barely have enough fuel to get back to the ship. We'll be below bingo when we get there."

An expletive or two followed before K-8 responded, "All right. Back to the boat we go. I'll take care of Noodle and get us to the ship. You keep working the fuel calculations—and let folks on the carrier know what's up. We'll need their help."

We would divide and conquer, switching roles and responsibilities so that K-8 was best positioned to support our pilot during what was turning out to be a particularly nerve-racking flight.

I took a deep breath and looked down at the bumblebee-yellow page in my lap, marked at the top with BINGO in a large, jarring font. It held a detailed chart of every data point we needed—altitude, airspeed, distance traveled, head winds, and more—to calculate how to conserve as much fuel as possible while flying back to the ship.

The adjacent page had instructions for ditching our jet in the ocean. Under the title was a note in bold black print that read: "Ditching the aircraft is the pilot's last resort."

A Shift in Focus

My entire school was invited to our local neighbourhood cinema to watch *Hidden Figures*, the award-winning film about three African American female mathematicians at NASA who helped put astronauts in space. In one of the most pivotal scenes,

What Girls Need

Katherine Johnson is finally allowed to join a critical planning meeting for the Space Task Group. By the end of the scene, we see her become the driving force for the developing of a new equation to help guide the astronauts' capsule back to Earth during re-entry from outer space.

I wasn't surprised that both our students and the teachers were enamoured with the movie's depiction of Johnson's strength and resilience. For the next week, I'd catch girls chattering in the halls about what they would've done in the same situation as Johnson and her colleagues—and whether they wanted to be a mathematician or an astronaut.

While that scene reinforces the movie's story of perseverance, hard work, and sheer gumption, it also reveals the unique perspective that these women brought to NASA's effort to put a man on the moon. Their approach to collaboration, while largely shunned because of their gender and race, was ultimately essential to fulfilling President Kennedy's vision and solving one of the most dynamic and complicated problems of the century.

As author Margot Lee Shetterly noted, in her book of the same title that provided the basis for the popular movie, there were so "many ways to screw the pooch, and just one staggeringly complex, scrupulously modelled, endlessly rehearsed, indefatigably tested way to succeed." One of the biggest hurdles for America's race to the moon wasn't necessarily the technical complexity of the task or a budget that required $20 billion in 1969 and 400,000 people. Instead, it was the massive amounts of coordination and teamwork, communication and conflict resolution, adaptability and flexibility, and distributive leadership styles required to get

Nurture Her Collaborative Problem-Solving Skills

the job done—all features of effective collaborative problem-solving. As Shetterly described it, the scientists, engineers, and mathematicians of the Space Task Group, including Katherine Johnson, had to "turn their desks into a trigonometric war room, poring over equations, scrawling ideas on blackboards, evaluating their work, erasing it, starting over." There was no way to find new solutions to intractable technical problems without developing new systems for collaborative problem-solving, too.

Fast-forward fifty years and you'll see that today's NASA has placed these twenty-first-century skills front and centre in the training programmes for its astronaut corps, engineers, and scientists. Jessica Meir, one of the eight members of NASA Astronaut Group 21, described this as balancing subject-specific expertise with the soft skills that prepare astronauts to tackle the complex challenges they regularly face in space. In a message sent from the International Space Station shortly after she completed the first all-female space walk in history, Meir explained the importance of what she called "creative problem-solving", saying, "Here in space, we use all kinds of skills to get our work done. Maths and science, of course, but also communication and teamwork—keys to making sure we stay safe and accomplish important tasks. Each day, we are working with the astronauts, cosmonauts, and ground teams from our partner agencies all across the globe on an incredible diversity of experiments and activities." In short, the ability to solve problems in teams is essential, in space and in life.

This emphasis even applies to how NASA now frames its education and outreach to schools, teachers, and students. In 2017, the space administration launched a new programme to connect schoolchildren with the International Space Station through tailored lessons for different age groups. One of the first modules, called "Expeditionary Skills for Life", showed parents and teachers how to help children learn that when it comes to solving problems, in outer space or on planet Earth, maximizing the input you get from multiple viewpoints creates a big advantage. Collaboration is key.

In other words, the focus has shifted. Today and moving forward, one of the most important lessons we can give our kids is teaching them how to problem-solve collaboratively from an early age.

Girls' Natural Advantage

By now, I hope you're convinced that the ability to solve problems effectively by working with two or more people to pool knowledge and find creative solutions is important—and will become even more essential to success, in and out of the workforce, over the decades ahead.

But what's the deal with the gendered aspect of this critical twenty-first-century skill? Does problem-solving in groups really look different for women and men, or for girls and boys?

Yes, it does. In fact, it's often where girls show natural aptitude and where boys need more help and training to be effective. Indeed, even while schools have yet to really emphasize teaching this skill, girls around the world are already showing that they're naturally predisposed to be better at it.

Nurture Her Collaborative Problem-Solving Skills

For evidence, consider a recent investigation by the Organisation for Economic Co-operation and Development (OECD) that surveyed 125,000 students in fifty-two countries worldwide. The study focused on measuring how effectively fifteen-year-olds solve problems when they are working with others. In particular, the team of researchers around the world looked at how students tackled problems when the solutions required "maintaining an awareness of group dynamics, ensuring team members acted in accordance with their agreed-upon roles, resolving disagreements, and monitoring progress towards a solution."

The results were in many ways surprising—surprisingly clear, that is. And completely in the girls' favour. When it came to collaborative problem-solving, girls performed significantly better than boys in every country, regardless of economic status and after normalizing for prior schooling in science, reading, and maths. On average, they scored nearly 30 points higher and were 1.6 times more likely than boys to be rated "top performers" at this essential twenty-first-century skill. This result was seen everywhere from Australia and New Zealand to Finland and Sweden, where girls scored over 40 points higher than boys in this area, to the United States and the United Kingdom, where the gender gap was closer to 30 points. What's more, the study showed that the relative size of the gender gap is even larger than for reading, which has traditionally been considered the area where girls outperform boys in almost every education system.

In other words, there is something about the approach girls take to communication, relationship building, and teamwork that makes them considerably more effective at collaborating to creatively find solutions when presented with problems. And this happens in spite of the fact that most schools aren't actively teaching these skills in their curriculum.

These findings also presented a stark contrast to an earlier study that focused on children's individual problem-solving skills. During that assessment effort, OECD researchers likewise identified a gender-based difference in skills—but it underscored that boys in general outperformed girls when it came to tackling problems alone.

Again, good news for our girls. Given changes under way in organizations and workforces around the world, which have responded to globalization and ever more complicated problems by becoming more team-oriented, the study suggests that young women are naturally "more able to cope with modern ways of working."

Our girls have the advantage at a skill that will become ever more important moving forwards. This is why collaboration is an ideal talent to promote when girls are young—so they recognize the importance of this natural behaviour and can effectively tap into it as adults, ensuring it becomes their lasting advantage no matter where they find themselves.

▌ What's Going On?

Why is it that, when that earlier study assessed individual problem-solving, boys showed a natural advantage—but when we emphasize the importance of applying multiple perspectives, experiences, and knowledge in group work, girls are more likely to succeed? And how can we help girls use this to their long-term advantage?

One answer lies in how girls and boys behave in small groups from a young age. For decades, social scientists and educators have observed the different ways that young children communicate with one another, noting how gender influences peer dynamics in and out of class. Take, for example, an early study conducted by researchers from the University of Minnesota, who monitored what happened when eighty four- and five-year-olds were divided into small groups according to their gender and given the chance to watch videos of *Snow White and the Seven Dwarfs, Cinderella,* or *Lonesome Ghosts,* another original, albeit less well-known, Disney movie. The trick was that their Fisher-Price toy movie viewer worked only if they collaborated. One child had to turn a crank to power the video and one had to hold down a button to light the viewer, while a third could view the cartoon through a viewing piece. The fourth child waited, hopefully patiently, for his or her turn.

After examining how long each group successfully managed to operate the cartoon, as well as the types of behaviour each girl and boy used to help the group solve the challenge of the problematic projector, it became clear that girls on the whole were more likely to use cooperative tactics to get Snow White, Cinderella, or the ghosts dancing across the movie screen. The girls were seen more often using specific accommodating verbal behaviours—requesting help from a classmate, offering to share access to the various roles, and showing concern for their peers.

Meanwhile, the boys defaulted to more competitive tactics, often using physical behaviour—touching, pushing and pulling, even attacking a classmate—to solve the problem at hand. While all the groups figured out how to watch the movie and no brawls broke out, the real-world experiment showed that by age four, girls and boys were already predisposed to solve problems very differently when in a group.

A later study echoed these results, while further exploring other subtle (and not-so-subtle) ways that young girls naturally collaborate with their peers. In particular, researchers noticed that girls were more likely to instinctively use verbal communication skills to find compromises or develop a shared plan with their peers—critical skills necessary for adults to effectively problem-solve in groups, too.

This follow-up research divided sixty preschool-aged children into pairs and asked them to complete two tasks. First they had to copy a Tinkertoy model laid out before them, and then they had to string together coloured wooden beads in a particular sequence—two very commonplace, entertaining tasks for four- and five-year-old kids. Every session was videotaped and studied for the verbal and non-verbal ways the students communicated to solve the "problem".

Girls in every group, whether working with another girl or a boy, used what the researchers called mitigating verbal behaviour more often, naturally working to solve the problem with their teammate by offering suggestions and compromises rather than controlling commands. Meanwhile, boys were more likely to work separately rather than work together towards a common objective.

Nurture Her Collaborative Problem-Solving Skills

Tellingly, in the all-boy pairs, each boy most often made his own Tinkertoy structure to complete the task, managing to individually solve the problem without collaborating at all.

Whether because of prescriptive gender stereotypes and group norms that unconsciously influence each of us from an early age, because of how young girls and boys interact with peers, or because how friends influence a child's social and emotional development, girls are more likely to be aware of relational dynamics when they take on problems. Similarly, when collaborating with other kids of their same gender, young girls are even more likely to prioritize mutually beneficial outcomes—an early sign of future potential effectiveness when it comes to collaborative problem-solving. In short, our girls are naturally predisposed to consider important social dynamics when trying to tackle challenges in a collaborative way, ultimately making them more effective at group problem-solving.

These studies not withstanding, I'm sure that some readers will still wonder if these conclusions are an overgeneralization, or just reflect what happens in a lab or controlled classroom environment. Does this happen in the real world, too?

To consider that question, let's take a brief look at another realm entirely—not outer space, but the world of conflict resolution and peacekeeping. The field of peacekeeping, which involves supporting civilians during conflict and moving groups of people away from warfighting and towards peace agreements, presents some of the toughest real-world problems imaginable. It certainly requires expert levels of collaboration, coordination, and nuanced communication. It's also a space that has historically not included women. From 1957 to 1989, only twenty women (in total!) officially served as uniformed peacekeepers for the United Nations. That's changed recently. As of 2017, women represent 22 per cent of the 16,500 civilian peacekeepers working with the United Nations, and more are involved with the police and military functions of this work.

Critically for our conversation, this change largely reflected a growing appreciation of how effective—and, in many cases, how essential—women are for peacekeeping operations. Both practitioners and researchers have seen this impact, noting how influential women are in modern peacekeeping efforts because of their ability to connect with locals, their approach to communication and collaboration, and their often unique approach to helping others, including opposing forces, discover areas for compromise even under the most difficult of circumstances. While it took years for women to be integrated into these sorts of dangerous operations, even those most resistant to women serving in this capacity couldn't ignore the positive results. Indeed, it's often the positive impact of this type of collaborative problem-solving that wins over those who are most opposed to having women doing this work on the front lines.

As the career educator who oversees Baldwin's middle school put it, "Girls are often more willing to talk and engage each other." While we talked, I could see her flipping through a mental Rolodex cataloguing thousands of hours with students, in and out of class.

"They like working together and connecting with one another, whether it's for schoolwork, a club, or in purely social moments," she continued emphatically. "It fulfills a young woman's need to belong."

I reflected again on my conversation with Jasmine, the confident and gregarious thirteen-year-old whose passion was Indian dance class and coding, even as her favourite daily activities include reading and teasing her younger sister.

We were talking about a recent project she'd completed for our school's technology club, where she'd worked with a group of students from different middle school years to develop a new video game. From start to finish, the project took over a year, but Jasmine was visibly bursting with pride when we talked about how well it went. Just the week before, the video game had been launched at an exhibition in Philadelphia, where college professors and computer scientists applauded the innovative ideas that Jasmine and her partners had brought to life on the gaming console.

When I asked why it went so well, Jasmine was momentarily perplexed. To her, it seemed obvious. "It's just something that we do," she explained. "I really like collaborating ... Honestly, if you have help from others, then it's much easier and it's also more fun."

Pausing briefly, she adjusted the zip on a small light pink backpack sitting by her side. "You know what I'm saying?" she implored.

Clearly I was still a step behind Jasmine and her friends. Collaborative problem-solving came naturally to them. I just hoped they learned to leverage this skill for maximum effect in the real world awaiting them.

What's a Parent to Do?

The good news is that there are immediate ways that parents and teachers can help girls nurture their intrinsic collaborative skills so they can fully embrace their talent for complex problem-solving in groups and hold fast to this skill when they're older. While you won't be able to do everything that we'll talk about in this chapter—nor should you feel pressured to try!—keep these ideas in mind and weave a few into your actions or into daily conversations with your daughter. Young girls are constantly responding to the indirect signals sent by society, peers, and family members. Even little things can make a big difference, so start small and go from there.

With that in mind, what areas are most important? What should we focus on? Let's start with what's going on at school. Consider what sort of learning environment your daughter has in class, or if you're a teacher, how you're setting the stage for collaborative problem-solving on a regular basis. Are the soft skills involved with this important talent, including effective listening, coordination, and teamwork, part of the curriculum? Are these elements described as goals for lessons so that each girl consciously understands the importance of these soft skills? If not, is this an area your school is working on—or if you are an educator yourself, can you find new ways to bring out these concepts more clearly in students' classrooms?

Both parents and teachers should keep in mind, of course, that it's not enough to simply introduce group problems into a

Nurture Her Collaborative Problem-Solving Skills

lesson or course. The solution isn't just to put girls in teams for an assignment and hope for the best. One of the most important steps to learning effective collaborative problem-solving is having adults facilitate children's work in this area. In other words, turning a science lab experiment that would traditionally be done alone into a partnered project is only the first step. Next, build on the actual time spent collaborating by having students talk about their ideas and debate not just the meaning of whatever results they find, but also how they coordinated on different parts. And help work together through the most difficult aspects of any project rather than defaulting to the "it's easier to just do on my own" approach.

Research shows that girls who are given opportunities to explain their ideas after working with partners or in a team setting increase their inclination towards and effectiveness at collaboration by as many as six percentage points. If there is a project under way in class, consider asking students to reflect with a friend on how it's going, what parts are fun, what happens when they hit roadblocks—and, as important, how they navigate rough patches with their partner. Parents can help by using the otherwise quiet car ride home with your preteen daughter not just to inquire "How'd the project go?" but rather to ask her to explain what ideas she contributed and what other perspectives her classmates provided. Or see if she will recount the funniest moment she had with the group when they were working together. This will help avoid the one-word responses typical of many preteens and teenagers and reinforce important collaborative problem-solving lessons, too.

What Girls Need

Another thing to think about is the makeup of the student body at your girl's school or, on a smaller scale, among her group of friends. Studies show that a more diverse peer group helps children become more effective collaborative problem-solvers and that exposure to diversity in academic settings is particularly helpful. Studying, playing, and lunching with peers from a wide variety of backgrounds and with a breadth of family experiences help children practise navigating difference early on, so they can learn to communicate effectively with others who may have different points of view. These early acts help develop essential interpersonal relationship management skills—skills that will prove invaluable when, as adults, they must help solve a complex problem with a team of colleagues, likely from around the world. Although as parents we rarely have control of these areas, it's still worth keeping in mind their benefit to a young girl's growth trajectory.

Your daughter's free time away from school can also reinforce these lessons. Extracurricular activities are particularly helpful here, especially those that actively encourage your daughter to work in a team and build self-confidence as she navigates the trials and errors associated with group-oriented collaboration. Encourage your daughter to join the band, the student newspaper, a team sport, or a volunteer activity, depending on what she is most passionate about. Many of these activities nurture collaboration or problem-solving, and even if the two skills don't naturally overlap in a given sport or activity, they still increase girls' positive attitudes towards this way of thinking and working.

Nurture Her Collaborative Problem-Solving Skills

Keep in mind that some extracurricular activities help more than others, even when they don't obviously focus on teamwork. For example, the OECD study cited earlier found a positive correlation between students' moderate physical activity—including individual activities like walking and riding a bike—and their ability to effectively problem-solve collaboratively. For teenage girls in particular, improvements were seen after just two days with about sixty minutes of moderate movement. So an easy way to help your daughter on multiple fronts, and especially with collaborative problem-solving, is to encourage her to take the dog for a walk, play a pickup game of football with friends, and ride her bike around the neighbourhood.

You're also no doubt thinking about the games your daughter plays in her free time. Do they help? Interestingly, the research is mixed concerning how games of all sorts—including video and board games—affect kids' learning. On one hand, games have been shown to be effective at teaching adolescent children different ways of thinking or working, including the soft skills we're talking about that support problem-solving and collaboration. By putting kids in a state of play, they make the process of trying new things, taking risks, and even failing—all things that girls, who generally exhibit more perfectionistic and risk-aversive tendencies, may try to avoid—part of the process and of the fun. Games can also help your daughter practise how to communicate with teammates and competitors, and how to work with others in challenging situations.

Still, as family game night approaches or you're selecting a game for your daughter's next birthday present, choose carefully. Some work better than others when it comes to building these important twenty-first-century life skills. For example, try a multiplayer role-playing game, many of which are based on the premise that players work together to tackle a challenge. One popular choice is Spirit Island, in which players collaborate to defend their home—an island of spirits, of course—from invaders. Any parent whose daughter rolls her eyes at role-playing might instead try the cooperative card game Cahoots, which is easy for young children to master but can be adapted for older players, making it ideal for preteens and adults, too. Another fun option is Telestrations, an updated version of Pictionary that creates more person-to-person interactions than the version we grew up with—making for a funny and creative take on the Telephone Game using pencils, sketch pads, and your imagination, and reinforcing the underlying practices of collaborative problem-solving.

Video games, an everyday part of life for many preteens and teenagers, are another area to approach with caution. Indeed, that same OECD study that investigated collaborative problem-solving around the world found a negative correlation between playing video games and the ability to collaborate. In large part, this is because online gaming makes it relatively easy to avoid the relationship-building aspects of collaboration that are so critical to this work in the real world.

That said, while encouraging your daughter to spend less time playing video games is an option, you'll find it easier and more practical to simply be aware of how much time she spends on this one activity and what video games she chooses to play most often. Simulation games, like the board games described above, and massively multiplayer online role-playing games, or MMORPGs, as they are more commonly known, are the most beneficial and can be fun ways to work on this important skill. They help encourage cooperation and competition on a large scale, are available in a wide variety of genres to suit your child's interests, and often involve real-world-esque problem-solving scenarios. More to the point, teens and preteens (adults, too!) love them.

That's why I wasn't surprised to see Jasmine's eyes light up when we started talking about her favourite activities at home. She launched into a description of the video games she plays with her sister, cousins, and neighbourhood friends. She noted that her dad sometimes insists on joining, too. Before long, she'd given a full rundown on her most recent round of *Overcooked! 2*, a video game that simulates unconventional cooking challenges and requires you work with up to three other players to cook a meal. Jasmine was particularly proud of how successfully she, along with her sister and two friends, managed to cook a pizza despite the roadblocks the game kept throwing in their way.

"It's really cool," she offered, her red-jean-clad knees bouncing as she described the various steps: chopping (virtual) tomatoes, preparing (virtual) dough and cheese, and coordinating with the other chefs across a barrier in the (virtual) kitchen.

"The game makes it fun to work together," she continued. "Then it all becomes sort of basic. Like crossing the street on your own."

"Like crossing the street?" I asked.

"Yeah, like stuff you do every day."

Jasmine turned to her eleven-year-old little sister, Pia, who'd joined her on the couch a few minutes prior. Pia squirmed a bit as her sister told stories; she was clearly proud of her older sister, though she was trying not to show it. She also wanted her chance to talk.

"It's like what happens when we're going into the city," Pia offered, her brown ponytail bouncing and her hands tucked under her legs to keep them steady. "We had to decide where to park and what side of the street to get out on.

"My mum is better with streets than my dad," she offered with a giggle and a shrug, "but I know some of the roads, too. They look familiar from this camp I went to every day. So it was easier for me to chime in. My mum always asks where I think we should go."

"So your parents actively encourage you guys to help them solve problems, like where to go in the city?" I asked.

"Yes! We kind of all put ideas into the problem," she offered. It was clear that her parents, perhaps unconsciously but none-theless effectively, were also modelling the lessons that we teach in class through their daily conversations and while playing games.

The two sisters' enthusiasm was contagious and made me ex-cited for what's to come. By the time they were in middle school, both Jasmine and Pia thought solving problems in teams, with all sorts of people and in both relaxed and challenging moments, was as "basic" as crossing the street or figuring out where to go in a crowded city. Yes, these are no doubt easy real-world problems. But they nonetheless helped these young girls practise sharing solutions, figuring things out while working in a group, and navigating challenging moments. Along the way, the sisters grew confident in their ability to problem-solve collaboratively. Despite the many hurdles they will one day face in the real world, both girls are now situated to more effectively use this natural ability.

Given the complicated realities involved with preparing our girls to succeed no matter what the future holds, it's comforting to know Jasmine and Pia will have this advantage.

O ver a decade later, I can still feel the damp weight of my sweat-soaked flight suit that night in the jet. I also remember the sense of efficiency and focus that overtook our cockpit. For the forty-five minutes that followed our failed refuelling attempt, K-8 and I divided and conquered tasks with smooth and easy communication, seamless coordination, and a mutual appreciation for what was at stake. And with an innate understanding of how best to support each other and our pilot, too.

She helped keep Noodle calm, navigated the plane back to the carrier, and talked with other jets in the vicinity of the ship even as she managed the numerous checklists related to in-flight operations. I kept updating our fuel numbers and tracking other systems on the plane, rechecking for emergency diverts as our location changed, and working via the radio with a team on the carrier to develop backup plans for the still-unfolding situation.

What Girls Need

In an attempt to keep the mood light, we intermittently cracked lame jokes and debated what midnight snack would be waiting in the mess after we landed.

The coordinated effort to safely land our jet soon extended well beyond our cockpit. Before long, it involved pilots in other airborne jets as well as fellow aviators in the carrier's air operations command centre, who helped clear the flight deck and restrict other planes from taking off or landing, to give our jet as much space, time, and latitude as possible to get back on board safely.

There was Radio, one of the friendliest F/A-18 Hornet pilots on the ship, who launched an emergency mission to rendezvous with our plane as we approached the carrier, in a second attempt to give us some extra fuel. There was Meat, one of the most seasoned pilots in our squadron, who talked us through the backup plan of all backup plans, which included putting a large barricade—really just a sturdy nylon net—across the flight deck, to catch the plane if we ran out of fuel and couldn't safely navigate a normal carrier trap. It was the sort of thing that happened aboard the boat maybe once every five years, if ever, but was still a better scenario than having to eject. And there was the landing signals officer, who helped talk Noodle through a failed bolter landing before we finally called "bingo on the ball"—telling the world just how dangerously low on fuel we were—and landed safely aboard the ship.

But when I now think back on that night, what stands out to me is the moment when K-8 and I effortlessly fell into roles that unknown to us were ours all along. When we shifted from being

Nurture Her Collaborative Problem-Solving Skills

inexperienced aviators who didn't know what to do next to being effective collaborative problem-solvers who knew they were well positioned to help the team—any team—figure out the answers. It's the feeling every young girl should have before she ventures into the world.

Make Empathy Her Natural Advantage

Waiting for Walid and Mohammed to arrive, I adjust my hijab one more time, tucking the thin silk headscarf a little tighter under my chin so that only the centre of my face is visible. In my long black abaya and matching headscarf, I almost pass for a Yemeni woman. Maybe the locals lounging in scattered chairs around the hotel courtyard won't notice me reading at a corner table. Maybe the men—only men at the outdoor café, as usual—won't wonder about a young woman sitting alone. There's little chance they'd realize there's an American in their midst, waiting to interview a former Al-Qaeda operative and his interpreter friend.

Walid enters the garden with a flourish, the hem of his white thawb—a traditional long shirtdress worn by Arab men throughout the region—kicking up dust behind him and his muted brown Yemeni scarf folded precisely over each shoulder.

What Girls Need

Mohammed, the interpreter, trails him slightly, scanning the clusters of Arab men in faux Pottery Barn wicker chairs alongside cherry-red umbrellas. I wave and they approach quickly, silently, with long strides and broad smiles.

"I did not think it was you, in the abaya and hijab. You could be Al-Qaeda!" exclaims Walid in a hushed voice, barely loud enough for our little group.

I laugh appreciatively, momentarily tempted to share the great bargain I got on my bedazzled robe and matching headscarf, purchased from a dirty Sana'a department store the week prior. Walid extends his hand in greeting, a surprising gesture for a former member of Al-Qaeda—whose members usually refuse to touch a woman who is not a family member, but especially a young American—then ushers me to a sitting area off to one side.

As a researcher visiting Yemen to study Al-Qaeda and local terrorist organizations, I am well aware that local government officials monitor my activity. Others with more questionable intentions likely track my whereabouts, too. It makes me appreciate the relative anonymity of my stifling but nondescript abaya and the disposable cell phone and new phone number that I picked up last week. Nevertheless, I still regularly update former law enforcement colleagues about my whereabouts and mentally review how to respond in a bombing or hostage situation. Just in case. Walid, a former terrorist, and Mohammed, a Yemeni military officer turned unofficial interpreter, are equally wary. It took days of back-and-forth—over where, when, and even if we'd meet—to arrange this informal breakfast meeting.

Make Empathy Her Natural Advantage

Perched on hard benches at the garden's edge, we're far from the handful of Arab men enjoying morning tea and the local *Al-Ayyam* newspaper. We can speak relatively freely about Walid's training with Osama bin Laden in Afghanistan and his thoughts on Al-Qaeda's more recent influence in Yemen, since the Arab Spring. He wants to share his story and have someone, especially an American who was previously a government official, appreciate his perspective. My hope is to better understand why teenage Muslims join local terrorist groups, like the powerful Al-Qaeda in the Arabian Peninsula, who were then waging a bloody war in southern Yemen. And to grasp how a young Yemeni finds himself in the harsh mountains of eastern Afghanistan, training with and swearing allegiance to Osama bin Laden. What motivates these men—and occasionally women—and do they really want to kill every American they meet?

So I plan to have breakfast with an ex-Al-Qaeda operative and hear his stories about life as a terrorist. Pen poised and pleasantries out of the way, I glance at my scrawled list of questions. "Walid, tell me about your time with Al-Qaeda. Why did you join Osama bin Laden in Afghanistan?"

It was a moment that demanded that I connect with someone across huge cultural and language divides, understand his perspective, and help him to appreciate my point of view, so that together we could explore how to address some of the most intractable national security challenges of our generation. It was a time when empathy was critical to my success—and indeed, my survival.

What Girls Need

As seventeen-year-old Eliza strides into the room, her white canvas sneakers squeak as she bounces across the polished wood floor. Her smile is contagious and her optimism is visible. Like many of her classmates, she is still basking in the glow of high school graduation. Her hands flutter as she talks about her summer thus far, eager to tell stories of her friends and her grand plans for going to university this autumn.

As we chat, Eliza reminisces about high school and shares her favourite highlights. Her smile falters only when a friend's name comes up and a sad memory comes to mind. "I've had classmates who've had to deal with unimaginable loss," she recalls, thinking of not just one but two friends who lost a parent when they were barely teenagers. "Being able to be there for them at funerals and times when they needed support..."

Eliza pauses, bites her lip, and I sense that she is picturing scenes from the memorial services in her head. "To try putting ourselves in their shoes," she continues, thinking about how her friends all responded to those tragedies. "All of us would send a text and say, 'If you need us, we're here.' No one shied away from that."

"Where did you learn that?" I ask, curious how Eliza and her friends learned to so effectively demonstrate empathy.

"It's something we've always done."

A second later, Eliza launches into a story from Year 6, involving a classmate who fell ill and was hospitalized. "I remember when she got sick," Eliza shared, fiddling with her phone as she pieced together the memories. "She was in a coma, but we were told she would react if she heard things. We took turns reading a book that she liked. Recording it on a tape they played for her, so she could hear us. It was a silly book, *Diary of a Wimpy Kid*, but it was her favourite."

"What a nice thing to do."

"One person suggested it," Eliza recalls. "We wanted to be there for her … I think that girls are more inclined to look out for one another and to try to understand where others are coming from."

Why Is Empathy So Critical to Our Girls' Future Success?

My chats with Walid and Eliza were worlds apart. But as I listened to the teenager tell her stories, I couldn't help but think about my conversation with the former Al-Qaeda terrorist that summer day in Sana'a, as well as dozens of other discussions I had in Yemeni and Saudi living rooms, Afghan homes, and the converted metal shipping containers that families call home at refugee camps on the Syrian border. In these situations, empathy was essential and helped me break down barriers, see things differently, connect with people, and in the process, discover new ideas.

As parents and educators, we typically think about empathy and its conceptual cousin compassion in terms of how they reflect our family values. Because being empathetic or compassionate is the "right thing to do". Or because the core elements of empathy—"the ability to understand another person's perspective; ... the ability to feel what someone else feels; ... [and] the ability to sense what another person needs from you"—sound a lot like the Golden Rule we all learned in nursery school.

So it's not surprising that when I'm chatting with Rachel, a soon-to-be Year 10 pupil who's known to friends and teachers as the kid who always shows concern for those around her, she tells me how her parents taught her to "treat people with kindness, no matter how they treat you." She explains that "it's important... just because."

On the one hand, I'm thrilled that this is her gut response. That she has internalized her parents' and teachers' lessons, and that she knows the importance of being kind. But I also want her to understand how empathy and compassion don't just touch others, but change her, too. And that the ability to effectively empathize is a tool she will need and want in the future, not just with friends and family. When I begin to explain why empathetic skills will be critical to her professional success as an adult, she looks surprised. Both by the notion of being old enough to be called an adult and by the idea that what Rachel describes as "little things that are simply a habit because they're good to do" matters more than she realizes.

It's easy to take empathy for granted as a good life skill. But by filing it away in the "good things to remember" folder of our minds, we don't adequately consider the many reasons why empathy is important to our girls' future success—or discuss how best to nurture empathetic habits throughout childhood. Over the past two decades, more and more attention has been paid to the role of emotional intelligence in and out of the workplace. During this period, social scientists have worked to quantify the benefits of empathy and to understand its influence throughout one's life. The research suggests that the ability to demonstrate empathy has an impact on everything from the state of your marriage to the effectiveness of your social media persona. Empathy is also essential to effective leadership in today's workplace, helping you "influence others in your organization, anticipate stakeholder concerns ... and even run better meetings." So it's not surprising that a 2011 study by the Center for Creative Leadership analyzed input from 6,732 managers from thirty-eight countries around the world and found that empathy is positively correlated with an individual's job performance. Another more recent study, by management consulting company Development Dimensions International, took this conclusion one step further. After assessing the leadership skills of over 15,000 executives from three hundred companies across eighteen countries, the firm's researchers concluded that in today's workplace, "empathy tops the list as the *most* critical driver of overall performance."

Beyond helping you manage relationships, engage your employees, and improve decision-making, empathy is also essential for creative thinking and innovation—critically important skills for success in the future workplace, no matter what industry you're in. That's why you may have recently heard CEOs from every sector imaginable—including tech companies like Microsoft, health-food companies like the snack maker KIND, and medical leaders like the Cleveland Clinic—trumpet how empathy has helped their companies and employees be more collaborative, more inventive, more customer-centric, and ultimately more successful.

That list includes Neil Blumenthal, the co-CEO of Warby Parker, the popular online retail company that sells prescription glasses and is valued at well over a billion dollars. When describing the cornerstone of Warby Parker's success, Blumenthal underscores their mission-focused approach to business and their core values, advancing the idea that employees should treat others—including their customers—the way *they* want to be treated. "Companies should be built to solve problems, and they should do that in a thoughtful way that takes into account customers, employees, the environment, and the community at large," he explains. It's as much about doing what's right for the world as it is about winning the race to recruit and retain top talent in your workforce. That's why empathic thinking is a critical part of work for every Warby Parker employee. Says Blumenthal, "I want our managers to care deeply about the people who work for them, to know a lot about each person individually and what motivates them."

Even more traditional businesses, such as the Ford Motor Company, have embraced this concept and are trying to increase their employees' use of empathetic skills in their daily work and approach to management. One estimate suggests that approximately 20 per cent of U.S. employers have recently added empathy lessons to their management training programmes, a significant increase from just ten years ago. At Ford, the aim is to improve the company's empathetic product design and ensure that their workforce understands customers' points of view when rethinking a car's design features. Shortly after joining the company, new engineers must squeeze into a specially designed outfit called an empathy belly, which helps them experience the realities of life as a mum-to-be as they test-drive various car models. The bulky fourteen-kilo ensemble, complete with fake breasts, a large faux belly, and a compression strap that wraps around your chest to simulate the shortness of breath felt by many expectant mothers in the third trimester, helps Ford engineers personally experience typical ergonomic challenges facing pregnant women. The goal is to ensure designers can empathetically design vehicles and create features that accommodate this subset of the company's customer base.

Putting empathy front and centre is also a central part of the business strategy that saved Lego, the legendary children's toy company. In 2005, then-CEO Jørgen Vig Knudstorp was tasked with saving the business, which had so lost touch with its core customers—namely, school-aged kids—that it was on the edge of bankruptcy. He launched a months-long project called Find the Fun, where ethnographers visited families in England, the United States, and Germany and spent the day observing play in action, shopping with children and parents at toy stores, and listening to them describe the social dimensions of playtime. The goal was to understand the wants and needs of today's kids. Among the outcomes were new products like LEGO Friends, a line of toys designed for girls that became a huge success. Corporations clearly get that empathy can be good for business, too.

For those readers still thinking that empathy is simply a

secondary soft skill that will be an afterthought in the future workforce, consider that the U.S. military also prioritizes it as a critical element to effective leadership. Reflecting decades of research and experience training soldiers, on and off a battlefield, American military officials decided to incorporate empathy training in one of their foundational leadership guides: the U.S. Army's Field Manual on Leader Development, FM 6-22. The nearly two-hundred-page tome, which describes the Army's view on effective collective and individual leadership, lists empathy among a leader's most important character traits—citing the ability of a strongly empathetic leader to influence those they are managing, members of the local community, and potential adversaries, too.

As Lieutenant General H. R. McMaster, who is well known for his leadership in combat during the Persian Gulf War and the Iraq War and, more recently, as White House national security advisor, told me, "empathy is essential to success on and off the battlefield. Understanding the emotions and aspirations that drive and constrain the other is the first step in defeating enemies, influencing neutrals, and galvanizing friends."

In short, empathy will be key to our kids' future personal and professional success.

W alid waits a few minutes to respond to my open-ended question about his time as an Al-Qaeda fighter, as a waiter takes our order. He and Mohammed discuss whether to get tea or lemonade and I scan our surroundings, which are oddly serene given that we're in the capital of a failing state and a war-torn country where terrorist attacks are a regular everyday occurrence.

At the centre of one of the nicer hotels in Sana'a, the courtyard is a welcome respite from the dust, noise, and ever-present threat of being kidnapped that are part of daily life on the streets of Yemen's largest city. It's also a glimpse into a Yemeni's vision of Las Vegas, albeit without the alcohol or the scantily clad women. Doing its best to replicate a luxury Western establishment, the hotel's garden boasts a surreal mix of fake grass and real, towering palm trees alongside a glistening unused pool with a small sputtering waterfall. Middle Eastern lift music plays in the background a bit too loudly, competing with the local mosque's call to prayer. Staff in ill-fitting black and red uniforms mill about, waiting to bring the few loitering guests overpriced coffee or tea. Only the occasional roar of military jets flying overhead and the multiple metal detectors guarding each entrance hint at the insecurity outside the hotel's high walls.

Our drinks on their way, Walid begins to describe how and why he joined Al-Qaeda in the 1980s and what it's like for the young men who are now pledging allegiance to Al-Qaeda or other local terrorist groups. "Even if these boys are not with Al-Qaeda, they are storage for Al-Qaeda's thoughts," Walid explains, using broken English to describe the ideological and security implications when hundreds of young Yemenis become radicalized. "The only solution must come from God."

What Girls Need

"Then I guess we can do nothing but sit and enjoy our lemonade," I retort, hoping that my poor attempt at a joke will not be lost in translation.

With a small smile, Walid pulls his hand from the pocket of his thawb, reaching across the small wicker table to give me a jovial high five. "Yes, we must enjoy our lemonade," he agrees, smiling broadly at having understood American humour.

Enjoying the banter, Walid decides to turn the tables and press me for information. The conversation shifts to a discussion about the influence of religion around the world. Walid asks about my spiritual beliefs. "Please explain, Miss Marisa. What religion are you?"

I shift in my seat and wave the question away. He repeats his request, assuming I'm Christian and curious about the different forms of Christianity in America.

I glance at Walid from under my headscarf, still tightly wrapped around my head from brow to chin, trying to read the look on his face. Stories of loss are written on the former terrorist's weathered skin, juxtaposed with the hope and humour in his gray eyes.

"I'm Jewish," I softly admit.

The words hang over our lemonade and cookies. I catch our interpreter, Mohammed, glaring in my direction, silently chastising me for sharing this dirty secret. Typically, it's not a good idea to tell a former Al-Qaeda terrorist that you're a practising Jew.

Girls' Natural Advantage

Given the importance of empathy for future success, it's natural to wonder how empathetic today's kids are. Unfortunately, research shows that today's young adults are largely less empathetic than prior generations. While children are still born with the capacity for empathy, efforts to nurture this behaviour and skill set seem to have fallen by the wayside recently. In fact, one study comparing college students in the late 1970s and early 1980s with their peers thirty years later showed, on average, a 48 per cent decrease in self-reported empathetic concern. This no doubt reflects changes in wider society that are beyond our control—things like increased levels of individualism, which by definition means people are less concerned with others, and increased materialism, which correlates to weaker personal relationships.

But there's also good news for our girls. As it turns out, there are gendered differences when it comes to empathy. More to the point, girls naturally demonstrate more empathetic tendencies from infancy—providing the foundation for a lasting advantage later in life, if we nurture this behaviour early on.

To help our girls most effectively, it's useful to first explore why evolutionary biologists, neuroscientists, psychologists, and social scientists think girls have greater natural abilities when it comes to basic empathetic thinking and action. Or, in the words of Simon Baron-Cohen, a psychologist at Cambridge University, what makes us think that "the female brain is predominately hard-wired for empathy". While such black-and-white statements—and related studies, which conclude that girls and boys, on average, demonstrate different empathetic skills within the first year of life—provoke passionate debate and raise as-yet-unresolved questions about sex-based behaviours, they also provide the basis for considering how biology interacts over time with culture and socialization to cement differences between women and men that continue into adulthood. Such differences can give our girls and future leading women an empathy advantage.

Take, for example, a 2013 study of primary school students in rural upstate New York. Keen to understand developmental differences in how kids respond to mixed emotional signals, a team of psychologists recruited 128 children, ranging in age from five to twelve years old, to watch a ten-minute clip from the movie *Robots*. You may not recall this particular Disney animated adventure, but it was so popular at the time that 96 per cent of the students involved had already seen the film—many, more than once. For those who remember nothing but sleeping through that particular cartoon at the cinema, *Robots* is about a young robot, Rodney Copperbottom, who sets off to the big city to become an inventor. In the study, participating children, 65 of whom were girls and 63 of whom were boys, watched a short clip that showed Rodney upset about leaving his parents but excited for the adventure ahead. Researchers hoped it would speak equally to boys and girls, and prompt empathetic responses as the kids saw happy and sad aspects of the movie—reactions that were drawn out by adult observers, who asked questions like "How did Rodney feel at the end of the cartoon?" and "How did the Rodney cartoon make you feel at the end?"

Make Empathy Her Natural Advantage

The goal was to measure children's emotional understanding of what they watched and test their ability to empathize with Rodney, the movie's protagonist. At the end of the study, it was clear that both gender and age helps predict empathetic ability. Girls reported understanding and experiencing Rodney's mixed emotions at a far greater rate than their male peers did, even as older kids handled these questions more adeptly, suggesting that both boys' and girls' empathetic skills improved with age. In other words, girls have a natural advantage in using this essential tool of emotional intelligence—and it's one that can be cultivated over time.

Another study conducted in Germany looked at empathy development in adolescence and over a twenty-three-year period. Over 1,500 kids were asked, at twelve, fourteen, and sixteen years of age, a series of questions that measured their emotional and behavioural response to others' emotions. They were also questioned about their reactions to scenarios like a friend being nervous or afraid of a school test. Follow-up interviews were conducted two decades later, when they were thirty-five, to measure each person's perceptions of their empathetic ability and to see what had changed. As was true of those primary school students watching *Robots*, the girls had higher levels of empathy than the boys, and in general, empathetic abilities increased over the course of adolescence. What's more, empathy in one's teenage years predicted higher empathy in one's adulthood—meaning that this gender difference continued throughout life. Similar results were also seen in studies of empathy among undergraduate medical students and in related work on gendered perceptions of altruistic behaviour, volunteer-ism, and generosity.

Animal lovers will be interested to hear that these findings are mirrored in studies of empathy across the animal kingdom, too. Research shows that basic empathetic behaviours, including sensitivity to other animals' emotional states and the provision of comfort to social partners—and also to rivals—in distress, are exhibited by monkeys, chimpanzees, and lowland gorillas, as well as by elephants and some birds. Even rats and mice show distinctively empathetic behaviours that suggest these animals would "come to the aid of others in need and attempt to help them." What's more, when scientists focused their research on sex differences, higher levels of empathy were seen in female ani-mals than in their male counterparts. The next time you're at the zoo's primate reserve, watch closely, and you'll see that the fe-male chimps are more likely to console distressed by-standers. They appear to understand the needs of other chimps and re-spond by providing tools or food.

Numerous studies by evolutionary biologists, psychologists, economists, and neuroscientists explore this gender dynamic playing out in schools, zoos, labs, places of work, and more. It's therefore not surprising that popular definitions of what it means to be "feminine" put empathy high on the list of desired quali-ties—as well as compassion, a closely related concept. For exam-ple, a 2008 Pew Research Center survey reported that 80 per cent of Americans think that in general women are more compassionate than men. A later Pew study, from 2017, also confirmed the influ-ence of social norms and cultural expectations at play here. When asked what society most values in women, the second most repeated answer—by 30 per cent of respondents—was the fact that women were "nurturing and empathetic". The only answer heard more often was physical attractiveness or beauty, while most participants thought society most values in men qualities like honesty, morality, and professional success.

What does this mean for our girls? Even as we work to make men—and boys—more empathetic and neutralize the imbalance of this gender dynamic, we also should recognize the advantage that our girls naturally have. And make sure that their empathetic habits serve them well moving forwards.

▌ What's a Parent to Do?

Fortunately, there is a lot that can be done to ensure that our girls develop their natural empathy into a skill that becomes a lifelong asset, personally and professionally. While genetic makeup and biological preconditioning play a role in a person's empathetic tendencies, empathy can be developed like any other character trait. In fact, one study of twins suggested that while 33 to 50 per cent of a toddler's empathetic behaviour likely reflects genetic predisposition, as much as two-thirds of a child's empathic nature depends on environmental cues and lessons taught early on. In other words, the ability to understand and respond to another person's emotions is a skill that is influenced as much as or more by nurture than nature. This gives parents, teachers, and the influential adults in a young girl's life a unique opportunity to ensure that her natural empathetic tendencies grow into a game-changing advantage later in life.

First and foremost, thread ideas of empathy into and model empathy during daily interactions with your daughter. In the words of psychologist Alan Sroufe, "you get an empathic child by being empathetic with the child." What does this mean exactly? Model empathetic behaviours and discuss what you're seeing, feeling, and doing along the way, even when your daughter is quite young. From an early age, kids pick up signals as to how parents, grandparents, and other trusted adults pay attention to and respond to the feelings and experiences of other people and begin mimicking those actions. This involves adopting a modified Golden Rule—updating the rule we all remember from childhood to reflect the empathic idea of doing unto others not as *you* would want, but as *they* would want—and then talking about what you're seeing and doing. Countless everyday moments can be useful here. Perhaps it's when you're discussing how to help a family member or you're struck by something in the news that prompts you to pause and imagine yourself in another person's shoes. A simple comment like "I'm thinking about what your aunt might prefer" or "This news makes me wonder how these people feel and what they need" helps you openly model empathetic thinking and perspective-taking when children are young.

Role modelling of empathetic behaviour also means actively pointing out when you see others exhibiting empathy and sharing with your girl how these acts made you feel and the impact these sorts of habits have on others. Rachel, the fourteen-year-old we met early in the chapter, vividly recalls her mum doing just that when she and her sisters were younger. In fact, that's the aspect she remembers most when describing what happened when the family car broke down once while her mother was running errands.

"My mum was at the supermarket and I was home with my sisters when her car died," she explained, describing the frantic text messages she received that night. Rachel was barely old enough to babysit her younger sisters, so it was a big deal when her mother's quick trip to get dinner turned into an evening home alone.

"She called my dad, to see if he could leave work to come home, since we were alone," Rachel explained. "That's when a stranger heard a snippet of her call and, without asking, came to help."

The anonymous man in the parking lot spent the next half hour fixing her mother's car. A total stranger saved the day.

"I got this beautiful text from my mum about it," Rachel shared. "And when she got home, after we got the groceries inside, we had a long discussion about empathy. About how this man was willing to take thirty minutes out of his night to help a random woman. Someone he would likely never see again."

"What did you remember most from that conversation?" I asked, hoping to explore how it all translated to Rachel's ten-year-old self.

"My mum came to my room. She does that every night when we're going to bed," she shared. "We talked about what happened, and I remember my mum saying that it was so powerful, to see this stranger empathize like that."

What Girls Need

The stressful evening in the parking lot became a lasting lesson in empathy, for Rachel and her younger sisters, in large part because of the conversation that unfolded after it was over. It's a good reminder that it's never too early to find moments to talk to your girls when you experience moments of empathy or see empathy unfold in daily life. Even a short conversation provides positive reinforcement and helps your child interpret what she's seeing or hearing, and it leaves an enduring impression about the importance of empathetic skills.

Beyond making a point of role modelling empathetic habits and talking about those behaviours when you see them in others, you should also expose your daughter to different viewpoints from an early age. The goal is to have her develop a natural curiosity about other perspectives so that she is comfortable with and practised at seeing others' points of view and can react with empathetic accuracy, meaning that she has the ability to correctly read others' emotions and intentions. This is especially important with regard to people whose life experiences differ from her own. This will make it easier, when she's older, to effectively empathize with co-workers, partners, and friends in any real-world context.

An effective strategy at any age is to encourage your daughter to read fiction, especially stories about girls or young women. Books provide an easy way for children to explore other perspectives, and if the stories include characters she could imagine as a fictional version of herself, they can be a low-stakes way for her to practise stepping into the emotional shoes of another person. Indeed, research has established a correlation between reading

Make Empathy Her Natural Advantage

narrative fiction and improved abilities to infer what other people are thinking in real life. Reading provides practice at understanding different perspectives and ultimately establishes the basis for empathic reasoning. There are plenty of options for late primary and middle school students—including books like *Persepolis, Stargirl, Inside Out & Back Again,* and classics like *Charlotte's Web,* for younger girls. Picture books for early primary children are also a fabulous way to open their minds to other perspectives; some standouts to consider are *Red: A Crayon's Story; Hey, Little Ant; The Smallest Girl in the Smallest Grade;* or Dr Seuss's well-known *Horton Hears a Who!* and *The Sneetches and Other Stories.*

These stories also give you the chance to engage naturally in a conversation about empathy by asking your daughter questions about what a character might be thinking or feeling as the story unfolds. When she's reading any book—whether or not it's fiction or has an empathy-focused story line—occasionally ask leading questions such as: What do you think the characters are feeling? What choices would you make if you were in the same situation? What help do you think they want from others? This helps any reading she is doing, for school or for fun, become an opportunity for informal, open discussions about empathic thinking. In fact, both Rachel and Eliza spontaneously recalled how reading influenced their thinking in this regard and taught them the value of empathetic habits. Unprompted, Eliza even retold the empathy-inspiring plot of *Esperanza Rising,* from a Year 8 English class, which still lingered in her mind six years later. This award-winning novel by Pam Muñoz Ryan tells the story of a young girl moving from Mexico to California during the Depression, and the challenges she and her family faced along the way. "It was the story about a girl living a life that none of us were living, in a different time and a different part of the country," Eliza remembered. "It painted such a vivid picture of a life different than mine ... and really helped us learn to see things differently."

Given how much time today's kids spend with digital technology, many parents and teachers also wonder how online tools, particularly video games, help develop empathy. Because social media and other forms of virtual networks used in online games can instantly connect us with people around the world, some social scientists have suggested that "the potential to experience empathetic sensibility and to take it to a global level is now within reach." That said, in reality, the video games and other online tools we use today are less than ideal for teaching empathetic habits. First, most video game creators do not have empathy in mind when they are designing a new game. So, while other skills can be honed in the online world, including competition and problem-solving, many of the most popular games do not help reinforce empathy.

What's more, online tools that connect us to others around the world often obscure many authentic personal touch points that allow kids to practise skills such as accurate perspective-taking or sensing what someone else needs—especially given the tendency for social media to reflect on one's most "perfect" (often made up) self. Online networks are therefore more useful as tools for sharing information than as a means of practising empathy.

Make Empathy Her Natural Advantage

In other words, be cautious about relying on technology to reinforce our girls' empathetic tendencies, although over time we could see the development of digital tools that help inspire habits of empathy in the next generation.

In short, our focus should be the sorts of real-world face-to-face interactions that help your girl hone this important trait. For example, try using community service as an active tool for building empathetic habits with your daughter. Studies show that getting involved in service projects helps children develop a sense of emotional connectedness and responsibility for others. It also helps teach kids how to turn empathetic feeling into action, a sometimes difficult step for school-aged children, who do not automatically know what to do when they feel concern for another person. Community service thus becomes an ideal way to help your child practise the full range of empathetic skills—from taking into consideration the perspectives of others and trying to understand others' emotions to learning how to use that understanding to guide their actions. Consider what service programmes at your local community centre, school, or place of worship might pique your daughter's interest—whether it's a clothing or food drive, making cards for veterans or the elderly, helping with shelter animals, or being part of a tutoring or mentoring programme.

And don't be overly concerned if your girl's busy schedule means community service will take place less often than you'd like. While making these sorts of activities a regular part of her schedule is great, especially since it helps your preteen or teenager create more authentic connections with others not like her, even intermittent participation in these sorts of service programmes is useful—particularly if you discuss what she's seeing and doing along the way. In the car ride to and from school or at the dinner table, ask your daughter questions like "What impact do you think the project had on the people involved? What do you think they were feeling before and after? What do you imagine they might need next?" The combination of the activities themselves and an open dialogue about what she is seeing, feeling, and doing will go far to nurture your daughter's natural empathetic tendencies. These small acts can have a big impact, helping ensure she holds on to this essential trait in school, university, and beyond.

I 'm Jewish" hangs in the hot, dry air.

I shift in the wicker seat, trying to appear nonchalant as I adjust my abaya to better cover some restless strands of hair that escaped from my ponytail and head covering. After what feels like an hour but is really a few seconds, Walid shrugs, seemingly unimpressed by my revelation. I exhale, and suddenly realize that I'd been holding my breath.

"I am now a Bahá'í," Walid replies with gusto, surprising both me and Mohammad, my interpreter. Since parting ways with Osama bin Laden and Al-Qaeda, he had joined the relatively young Bahá'í Faith—a belief system that originated in Persia in the mid-1800s and emphasizes the spiritual unity of mankind. As a member of the Bahá'í Faith, Walid now believes that all the world's major religions are fundamentally aligned in purpose.

Make Empathy Her Natural Advantage

"Have you been to Jerusalem?" he wonders aloud. "Have you seen the Bahá'í temples there?"

Walid's new dream is to see the holy sites in northwest Israel that are destinations for Bahá'í pilgrims. As a Yemeni and a former terrorist, he will likely never be able to make the trip; the travel is too difficult and expensive, and his visa application too likely to be rejected. Perhaps, as a Jew, I could help him see the holy sites through my eyes. Though disappointed to hear that I hadn't seen the temples, Walid takes it as a small symbol of unity.

"No one can hurt you even if you are not Muslim," he offers, extending his hand in a gesture of good faith to his new Jewish friend. "The whole world is one."

As it turns out, former terrorists can teach lessons in empathy, too.

6

Her Ability to Adapt
Will Be Key

As I sank into the barber's tall swivel chair, tears started to well up in my eyes. Again.

I'd spent the past thirty minutes standing at attention in the hall outside the naval base barbershop, trying not to cry. Crossing my eyes so I wouldn't blink and hoping that I could keep the tears hovering on the edge of my lower eyelids from spilling down my cheeks. A small part of me welcomed the distraction, which helped block out the military trainers shouting at us.

It was my second day as a Navy midshipman, my first day in uniform during a week of indoctrination training that was meant to mirror boot camp. I was seventeen years old, three months out of secondary school but not yet a first-year in college. I was miserable but determined. I was also frightened—by the new demands of a nascent military career, by the move away from friends and family to start college, and by the general uncertainty of what was to come.

What Girls Need

The barber turned to look at me, the last of that morning's clients from the class of new officers in training. I caught the surprise in his eyes: I was the only girl in the group of male midshipmen who'd marched across base to his shop for a "welcome to the Navy" haircut. The other eight or so girls in our training class stayed behind in the dorm; the gunnery sergeant had decided their hairstyles followed military regulations, so they were left to shine shoes in silence. The barber was no doubt also surprised to see a midshipman on the verge of tears over a haircut, the most benign activity during the first week of military training.

Then he noticed the scars on my scalp, curved lines that extended about fifteen centimetres on each side of my head, from over my ears to the base of my skull. The incisions had healed just enough to turn from blush-red scabs to glossy white scars, barely covered by few centimetres of soft brown hair. The hair at the back of my head was still a few centimetres longer, as if it had been left untouched when the top of my head was shaved. The result was a quasi-mullet reminiscent of Kevin Bacon's hairstyle in the movie *Footloose*.

The story left unspoken was about an accident three months earlier, two weeks before my high school graduation. About a car that swerved and flipped over, trees that stopped the vehicle's forward motion, and an airbag that didn't deploy. About emergency responders who used the Jaws of Life to cut me from the car. About eight hours of surgery to remove blood pooled on my brain, five days in a medically induced coma, and another week in the hospital's intensive care unit.

And about the kind nurses who tried to preserve a small part of my girlish identity and shaved only the top of my head prior to brain surgery, leaving the long hair at the back of my head intact. Shoulder-length locks now grazed the back collar of my new Navy uniform—a violation of military grooming standards that triggered this compulsory visit to the barbershop.

As the barber shaved off the last traces of my long brown hair, a tear rolled down my cheek. He pretended not to notice.

S miling broadly, Sarah Robb O'Hagan bounded into the café, her energy obvious as she skilfully navigated the shop's tightly set tables. I'd protected a prime spot at the back of the packed coffee shop, fending off groups of twos and threes who were gathering for mid-morning caffeine. After ordering pastries and coffee, we quickly launched into the sort of life updates that blur the lines between female colleagues and female friends in the best way. First came the latest stories about Sarah's preteen daughter and two teenage sons. Then we commiserated about juggling work and kids, the trials and tribulations of social media in middle school, and the difficulty of finding time to exercise.

With coffee refills on their way, our conversation shifted to Sarah's newest challenge—a professional leap so massive and risky that just hearing about it made me crave a second chocolate croissant. In the few months since we'd last spoke, Sarah was reinventing herself. She'd stepped down from her job as CEO of Flywheel Sports, the national fitness company known for its health clubs and high-energy spin classes, to launch a start-up called Extreme YOU.

What Girls Need

"So many times in my career, I have stood at that fork in the road, where I had a very comfortable option and a much riskier one," she had shared in an interview shortly after leaving Flywheel and life in the corporate world to become an entrepreneur. "[Whenever] I made the choice to take a bigger risk and get out of my comfort zone, I found it so much more rewarding."

Inspired by this approach to embracing change, I asked about Sarah's many career transitions, from working as a senior executive in the airline industry to overseeing marketing for a video game company to becoming one of the most powerful women in the sports industry. I saw her smile grow and her excitement build while she talked about her professional path. As Sarah's knee bounced under the small table with barely restrained energy, I had a fleeting vision of her leading a workout session right there in the café.

Sarah reminded me that she'd been fired twice, early in her career. Once, the combination of her quick termination and her status as a New Zealander meant that she lost her visa and was nearly kicked out of the United Kingdom. She also described the chaos of moving three times in four years, while she was at various stages in her pregnancy or right after her baby was born, because work demanded that she relocate across the country and back again. Sarah is as proud of surviving those and other moments of uncertainty and change as she is of her successes as a senior executive at Nike, then as the global president of Gatorade, and later as the CEO of Flywheel.

"It's the obstacles that help me grow the most," Sarah said. "You don't know how resilient you are until you are truly tested."

Her Ability to Adapt Will Be Key

That autumn, during the first assembly of our school year, a handful of students spoke to the entire school about their vision of the future. We'd encouraged them to picture the world as it would be in twenty or thirty years' time—to think further out than their next test or our upcoming homecoming weekend, and to mirror programming that our teachers were planning about the future of work. You heard a little bit about that opening assembly in the introduction to this book, when I shared Year 9 Kara's concept of life after college.

I was so inspired by Kara's comments that a few months later, I grabbed the chance to ask her about her speech and, in particular, to find out how she'd chosen her dream jobs. As we talked about her plans to be an "air and toxin researcher who figures out how to make air cleaner" or "instead of just being president, be someone who went between countries and helped them work together", I suddenly wondered aloud what makes her nervous about the future, about the plans that she seemed to have such a clear picture of.

Without a pause, Kara replied, "Control and stability."

I was momentarily stunned. The clarity and certainty of her answer didn't seem to fit with the thirteen-year-old girl sitting in front of me, pulling on the cuff of a pink sweater covered with small images of Santa Claus. When I asked her to elaborate, I smiled to hear her mature response, tinged with a teenager's view of the world.

"In school, there are answers. But at work, you might start a project and there may never be an answer. You may never get there. It's not like a lab in science or a report in history class, where you have control over what you do."

She paused to see if I was following her and understood what control and stability looked like in her mind.

"When you're an adult, you have to figure out what to do," Kara continued. "You're always doing new things. Maybe you're changing jobs or moving, or you're not happy and have to try something new.

"That's so risky. Especially since there is no one watching out for you, like your mum. It's like finding what you need from thin air."

When I recall my conversations with Sarah and Kara, or when I pause to remember my own winding path, the first word that comes to mind isn't adaptability. I'm more likely to think about resilience and grit, or to consider ideas like confidence, growth mindset, and risk-taking.

But recently a new theme emerged in research about the future awaiting today's students and in my discussions with parents and teachers about how we prepare the next generation for success. I keep hearing one word time and again: change.

I overheard a mother lament the swift transformations she's seeing in her own field; she is concerned about how the fast pace of change will impact her young daughter. And a teacher commented that "so much is changing in the world these girls will enter after they graduate", and then listed the things she wanted to add to her class curriculum to prepare her students for this new future. I heard a secondary school student note that "the world will change by the time I need a job", and a middle schooler say that "life is constantly changing and throwing curve balls."

And I spoke to a friend, Kate Shattuck, who is an executive recruiter for Korn Ferry, the largest headhunting firm in the world, with years of experience building effective leadership teams for companies around the country. Our conversation about the most critical skills for future leaders made clear that change is on her mind, too. At the top of the list of attributes she looks for in a strong candidate is the ability to adapt to change. In her view, the key to success is "knowing what to do when you don't know what to do ... adapting to new problems that we don't yet know exist."

With these comments in mind, I revisit my conversations with Sarah and Kara with fresh eyes. Sarah Robb O'Hagan needed to be comfortable with uncertainty when she left the security of her powerful CEO position to launch a start-up. She needed confidence in her ability to manage change when, early in her career, she was fired from not one but two jobs. She also needed to be skilful at adapting when her twins were born and she had to adjust to the roles of senior executive and new mum. Kara needed to rely on her natural adaptive talents when she moved not once or twice but seven times before Year 7, requiring multiple transitions to new neighbourhoods, new schools, new friends, and more. She also needed these skills when she switched instructors at dance class; she quickly concedes that this wasn't really such a big deal but also admits that, when she was younger, "my teacher would change and I hated it."

What Girls Need

My own adaptive skill set has been tested time and time again, too. A car accident in high school shook my self-image, altered my college experience, and nearly disrupted my long-planned path into naval aviation. Years later, my decision to stop flying abruptly ended my Navy career and sent me careening into uncharted professional waters. After some furious paddling, I committed to a different sort of national service and found myself travelling the world to study and coordinate counterterrorism strategy, navigating the uncertainty and emotional stress that came with solo research in war zones and failed states, like Afghanistan and Yemen. A decade later, I rejoined the school that started it all and where my self-image was first conceived, taking on a whole new set of personal and professional challenges and uncertainties as the school's head. Throughout, I thought that what mattered most as I navigated these twists and turns was grit combined with a sprinkle of feistiness and a dash of old-fashioned luck. I didn't realize that the trait that made the biggest difference was my ability to think flexibly, adapt to new places and new people, and be comfortable with massive amounts of uncertainty and change.

Being adaptable has been my lifelong advantage—the skill that made the biggest difference at work and at home. But it's also one of the hardest behaviours to learn. Only after years of trial and error did I feel comfortable flexing my adaptive muscles, so to speak. If we take into account the rapid shifts that are under way in society and the wider world and, in particular, the challenges that women will face in the decades to come, adaptability will be one of the greatest advantages we can give our girls.

■ The What and Why of Adaptability

In the simplest terms, adaptability is your capacity to respond to change and adjust to new situations as they arise. Although the concept is related to resilience and the ability to recover from difficulty, being adaptable doesn't necessarily mean that you're reacting to adversity or hardship. In fact, we most often rely on adaptive behaviours when we respond to the sorts of normal changes and moments of uncertainty that are part of everyday life—and that have become a defining quality of living in the fast-paced, ever-changing twenty-first century. These are ordinary challenges like moving or switching schools, starting a different job or special project at work, dealing with a new boss, a new software system, or even a new digital tool. On a more personal note, adaptability means adjusting to milestones like getting married or divorced, gaining new siblings or step-siblings, having and raising kids, getting a pet, losing a family member, and so on. All of these moments require adaptability, which the American Psychological Association defines as the "capacity to make appropriate responses to changed or changing situations; [and] the ability to modify or adjust one's behaviour in meeting different circumstances or different people."

While life has always demanded some degree of adaptability, recent trends in the workplace and wider society mean that to-day's kids will need this skill more than any generation that has come before. In fact, the ability to adapt may be one of the most critical drivers of personal and professional success for the 2.46

billion young adults of Generation Z and the still-to-be-named generations of children that will follow in their footsteps.

Why is this skill set gaining importance? First, consider the seismic impact of still-emerging technologies, including advanced robotic and artificial intelligence, big-data analytics, and the growing use of tools that blur the lines between the physical and digital space—things like wearable health monitors, self-driving cars, or even that Nest thermostat on your wall. This so-called Fourth Industrial Revolution will continue to alter our daily life at multiple levels and significantly impact how we work, relax, and relate to one another. The future will look very different than it does today, in terms of both what careers our kids will pursue and how they will work. As many as 65 per cent of the jobs that today's primary school students will one day hold don't yet exist, and the rise of new ways of working—including phenomena like the gig economy, which has recently created a massive increase in freelancers, small-business owners, and flexible workers—means that even the nature of our kids' workdays will be different. What's more, studies show that schoolkids are showing increased interest in pursuing entrepreneurial ventures, and that over the course of their lives, they are likely to change jobs more often than their parents' or grandparents' generation did.

All of this will require new skills, new ways of thinking, and new ways of navigating the world. Moving forwards, adults will need to constantly learn (and relearn) how to successfully deal with different technological advances, more novel situations, and the increased unpredictability that will be an inherent part of any career. To prepare for that reality, today's students must learn to be flexible thinkers, confident in their ability to adapt to the latest systems, comfortably adjust to new environments, and learn new skills quickly.

For an example of how this feels in the real world, consider recent analysis by the *Harvard Business Review*, which surveyed 682 business executives and senior or mid-level managers around the world to gauge how digital technologies will impact work over the next few years. The respondents, largely from manufacturing, technology, financial services, and utilities companies, stressed the importance of "change management capabilities" and disputed the popular notion that technical talent or technological knowledge are the most important skills for the future. Rather, the "ability to adapt to change" was deemed most important. These findings are echoed across nearly every industry, from tech startups and small businesses to the corporate world, and across all levels of the workforce. As General Stanley McChrystal, former leader of the U.S. Joint Special Operations Command and the commander of all military forces in Afghanistan during my time there, succinctly explained, "[B]eing effective in today's world is less a question of optimizing for a known (and relatively stable) set of variables than responsiveness to a constantly shifting environment. Adaptability ... must become our central competency."

This demand for flexible thinkers and adaptable leaders is already shaping how companies, non-profit organizations, and the world's leading employers screen for the next generation of C-suite leaders. Kate Kohler Shattuck, the seasoned executive recruiter I mentioned earlier in this chapter, described this priority as an increased need for "learning agility" and people with a "desire to want to adapt". "The larger trend impacting the future of work is not about solving any one new problem," she explained. "It's about handling the technological advancements that we have no idea are coming... About figuring out how to lead a team when there is a new problem that's never come up before." In fact, her firm is so keen on finding adaptable leaders that the tool they use to assess candidates for senior executive positions specifically screens for and measures nimble thinking, crisis management skills, tolerance for ambiguity, curiosity, and other key drivers of a person's adaptability.

For our girls, this demand for cognitive flexibility, creative thinking in the face of change, and confidence when dealing with uncertainty is heightened by a defining feature of life for many adult women: the realities of parenthood and the added complexities of being a parent who works outside the home. In discussions about preparing today's kids for the future world, we often discount this piece of the puzzle—particularly when we're talking about girls and boys together, or thinking about our daughters in the context of a co-educational school. There are no doubt advantages to this way of thinking, including how it helps us model for our daughters what gender equity might look and sound like. But we also know that motherhood introduces a wide variety of physical, emotional, and psychological changes unique to women. And more and more mothers are entering the work-force, even while their children are still infants and even as we continue to debate what it would look like for parents of both genders to equitably share child-rearing duties. As any mum will admit, this all means that the ability to be flexible and effectively respond to uncertainty and change is a prerequisite for life as an adult woman.

If success for the next generation will rely on not just your IQ (intelligence quotient) and your EQ (emotional quotient) but also the new concept of AQ (adaptability quotient), and if young women will need to adapt to change and handle uncertainty more than their male peers, the pressing question becomes: What now? What do our girls need most, when they're young, to be their most adaptable selves?

As the president of DreamWorks Animation, Margie Cohn leads one of the most well-known and well-regarded animation studios in the world. Given the popularity of movies like *Shrek, How to Train Your Dragon,* or *Kung Fu Panda,* almost every school-aged kid and many of their parents are devoted fans of the studio's work. Given her visionary efforts to reimagine the female protagonists that DreamWorks Animation depicts on the big and small screen, Cohn is also a reason why our daughters now have more spirited, sassy, and just-right-for-girls heroines to look up to. In other words, she is among the most influential women in Hollywood and defines more young girls' views of the world than almost any other C-suite executive.

She's also intimately familiar with how essential adaptability is to success.

"Nothing stops changing," Margie tells me, sharing stories of the leadership transitions she has navigated throughout her career, the evolution that took place when she had her two children, and the seismic shifts that currently influence the business side of the animation and movie industry. "In order to succeed and keep your sanity, you have to adapt to all of that."

Before long, she is recounting the behind-the-scenes story of how a team of DreamWorks animators developed *Spirit Riding Free*, a television series about a girl who moves from the city to a small town (managing change!), where she finds new friends (adjusting to new situations!) and tests her limits through daring adventures (handing uncertainty!). At the forefront of producers' minds was the feeling that it was time for girls to have their own adventure series, filled with challenging situations where the heroine had to handle and adapt to extreme change, so that girls in the audience could role-play what they would do in similar, albeit fantastical, situations.

It's no wonder that when Cohn describes what today's girls need most, she is clear about what the future demands. "It's imperative to take risks and have your voice be heard," she explains. "[But] if you can't adapt to change, you put yourself in a box . . . You have to figure out who you are and how you like to work with change. You have to be adaptable, to determine your new place and value in a new environment."

What Does the Research Say About Adaptability?

Unlike some of the other topics that we've discussed thus far, including competition and empathy, the study of adaptability is a relatively recent area of focus for researchers. Only during the past two decades, as social scientists explored how emotional intelligence—or as some might call it, social smarts—helps you monitor and respond to your and others' feelings, has attention turned to how an individual's social intelligence helps her navigate change in the modern workplace and life beyond, including transformations that are a result of globalization and rapid technological advancements.

To explore this question, social scientists built on earlier studies of adaptation at the macro level, which looked at how companies or organizations adjust in response to external environmental demands. These researchers analyzed real-world data, self-assessment surveys, and various experiments to explore why some people react well to outside stressors and why some people struggle with change more than others. In particular, psychologists, economists, social workers, and even military planners wanted to better understand how people manage change and uncertainty at work, how one's ability to adjust to a shifting environment impacts job performance, and what training helps people improve their adaptive skills. Concepts like adaptive performance and adaptive expertise soon sprang up, as did studies that helped people assess their or their employees' talent for adaptation.

One of the most comprehensive of these early studies was led by a team of organizational and industrial psychologists who wanted to develop a model of adaptive performance that could provide a baseline for predicting workers' adaptability across various industries. In other words, they wanted to define what effective adaptability looked like in action. Led by Elaine Pulakos, a renowned scholar in the field of talent management, the group collected stories from people holding twenty-one different types of private sector, military, and government jobs—from lawyers and executive assistants to air traffic controllers and state police troopers. After analyzing nearly 10,000 descriptions of what they called "critical incidents" common to these roles, researchers chose to study a subset of 1,311 challenging situations that required adaptive behaviours. The goal was to determine exactly how people in those roles altered their actions to respond to these specific novel, dynamic, or changing situations. Eight dimensions of individual adaptive performance were identified as key variables that impact real-world adaptability. These included the ability to handle work stress, solve problems creatively, deal with uncertainty, learn new ways to perform a job or task, and adapt to the cultural demands of a group or organization. While detractors argue that this model for defining adaptability is context-specific and oversimplifies some of the psychological and emotional aspects of the trait, it still provides a useful starting point for discussion—and a laundry list, of sorts, for the types of skills our kids need to become adaptable superstars when they grow up.

Of course, since we're most concerned about children, it's natural to wonder what these adult moments of adaptability look like at a young age. What adaptive skills come most naturally to kids? And what behaviours should we nurture if we want to encourage our girls' capacity to adapt?

A group of researchers at the University of Sydney set out to answer these questions by investigating the connection between adolescents' adaptability, personality, and academic

Her Ability to Adapt Will Be Key

performance. Turning their attention to preteens and teenagers at nine schools across Australia's east coast, they surveyed 969 students from middle and senior schools—which, in Aussie terms, means that about half were eleven to fourteen years old, and the rest were fifteen to nineteen years old. The survey asked the kids to rate themselves on how they dealt with new or uncertain situations, and their responses were analyzed to identify skills essential to students' (and adults', for that matter) adaptability. The results underscored specific ways of behaving, thinking, and emotionally responding that help a young girl or boy adjust in response to unforeseen changes.

As an example, consider how your daughter might respond when she forgets her house key and returns from school to a locked empty home. One indication of behavioural adaptability is how and whether she immediately takes action in response to this new and unanticipated situation. Is she is frozen by indecision and anxiety or do you return home to find her hanging out with a trusted neighbour instead? Cognitive aspects of adaptability include how one adjusts one's thinking to address changing circumstances or uncertain situations. In the context of this story, your teenager might plan for the next time she returns to an empty house by figuring out where to safely stash an extra key. Finally, this study demonstrated that the most adaptable students had developed a high capacity for emotional adaptability. In other words, they could manage the complicated emotions that come with change, novelty, or uncertainty. In our example, it's in how effectively your daughter quashes the natural fear and apprehension that comes in those moments.

What Girls Need

What's more, this team of Aussie researchers also found that a child's adaptability was directly related to how well she did in school—and beyond. Adaptable girls and boys were likely to participate more in class, enjoy school more, have higher self-esteem, and even demonstrate a greater sense of purpose. The ability to effectively adapt proved to be a game-changer for these students, in more ways than you might think.

Nine years after my visit to the naval base barbershop, my hair once again fell a few centimetres below my shoulders. I hastily twisted the ends in a knot and, with the black elastic tie always found on my left wrist, crudely fastened a low bun. It was a mostly futile effort to ensure my hair was above the collar of my flight suit, per the Navy's grooming standards. But after three-plus hours in the jet, the padding of my snug helmet giving me the textbook definition of "helmet head", there was little chance my hair would cooperate. Fortunately, because we were a week into this latest stint at sea, no one on the aircraft carrier would likely care about my messy hair.

I gave up on the bun, and after stashing my helmet on a nearby hook, I started to pull off the rest of my safety gear. I loosened the harness across my chest and inner thighs and stepped out of the webbed equipment that would hitch me to a parachute if I ejected from the jet. I peeled off the safety vest zipped tightly against my chest, handing it to a young tech standing by to check the signal flare, emergency beacon, sheath knife, and other survival equipment in its many pockets. Then I shimmied out of the G-suit trousers snugly fastened around my legs and lower abdomen, which would inflate when the jet did extreme manoeuvres to prevent my brain from starving for blood and keep me from passing out.

As I hung the last bit of fourteen kilos of safety gear in my locker, the muscles in my back relaxed and my headache started to subside. Our longer-than-usual flight had gone relatively well. We'd even finished the training portion with enough extra fuel to "cloud-surf"—which meant ten minutes aggressively banking the jet between cotton-candy shaped clouds, as if we were riding the ocean waves far below on a surfboard. Still, landing a jet on the deck of an aircraft carrier at sea was always challenging, always dangerous, and always tense. Particularly when the flight in question was one of your first flights with Bench, the squadron's commanding officer. Even when the boss wasn't watching, carrier landings were like trying to thread a needle while riding a unicycle.

As if reading my mind, Bench turned from his locker a few metres away and cleared his throat. "Chopper, what happened up there?" he said, glancing in my direction as he gathered the last of his flight gear in a camouflage-green bag at his feet.

"What do you mean, sir?" I replied, nervous that my boss was questioning my performance on that afternoon's mission and worried that my mentor was disappointed in me.

"You weren't you," he continued. "The last thirty minutes of the flight, you seemed off. You went quiet. You missed radio calls from the carrier, and you didn't talk me through our landing like I expected."

What Girls Need

I paused what I was doing, caught off guard. Two other aviators from my squadron hurriedly stowed their flight gear, pretending not to listen to our conversation.

"We're training for combat up there," Bench continued, his tone changing from boss to mentor. "I need to know I can count on you in an emergency or if we're over enemy territory. What's going on?"

I weighed my options. Should I blame a headache or explain the full story? Should I make up something dull or share details that only a handful of friends and colleagues knew?

"Sir, sorry if I was off up there," I responded, glancing at one of the other navigators in the room, a friend who knew my story. He shrugged subtly but supportively, then gathered his stuff and left the equipment room.

"Truth is, I was just trying not to get sick."

"What?"

"I was trying not to puke, sir," I continued. "Since day one of flight school, I've fought serious airsickness. It's been a thing my entire time in training, in the squadron, on deployment. My body never fully adjusted to our jet. But I can handle it. I can do what needs to be done."

"Who knows?" asked Bench.

"Just a few friends. The guys I flew with on our last deployment... I can manage it, sir. I always have."

Bench grew quiet and didn't respond until a few hours later. We'd finished a post-flight debrief, grabbed dinner, and were back in our squadron ready room when he called me over to the small standing desk he worked at while at sea.

"You know you don't have to fly," he said without preamble.

I stared at him and started to respond, but nothing came to mind. Bench kept talking to fill the silence.

"Chopper, if flying isn't for you ..." he continued, searching for the right words. "If you're getting airsick years later, you don't have to fly. There are other ways to serve."

Bench could see the confusion and trepidation in my eyes. I'd spent my young adult life working, scrambling, and fighting to fly for the Navy. To serve the military in this particular way. To perform this week's work on the aircraft carrier and prepare for my second deployment with our squadron.

"Marisa"—Bench dropped my call sign and, for emphasis, used my proper name—"I will support you either way. If you want to gut it out, that's fine. You can get through the next six months of missions on deployment and we'll figure out what happens after that. Or you can do something else for the Navy. I will support that, too."

He paused to let his message sink in. Then he said kindly, "Maybe it's time to try something different?"

▌ What's a Parent to Do?

The good news is that adaptability can be taught. While some features of your girl's personality make her more receptive to adapting—for example, if she's naturally open to new experiences or predisposed to take risks—adaptive performance can also be nurtured. Studies show that the traits and behaviours needed to more effectively respond to change and uncertainty can be readily fostered in both kids and adults. The key to supporting adaptability is to remember that small things make a difference and that perfection isn't the goal. In fact, the pursuit of perfection is actually damaging to your daughter's growth as an adaptive thinker, one who is buoyant in the face of change and uncertainty. What's important, instead, is to consider how we provide the sort of psychological, social, and practical supports that positively influence girls' capacity to handle the ambiguity that will define her adulthood.

First and foremost, encourage your daughter to practise embracing change and grow accustomed to handling new and different situations. The goal is to help her get used to the feeling of discomfort that comes with uncertainty and, with your guidance, develop her personal style for dealing with it. Many of the life changes that bring high levels of ambiguity and, as a result, feelings of unsteadiness are unplanned, such as when you need to move for a job, when your daughter's change in age means a change in schools, or when a sudden illness hits close to home. While these moments naturally provide the chance for your daughter to practise adaptive behaviours, they also bring emotional burdens for everyone involved. You may find it hard to imagine consciously using these opportunities to shape your girl's adaptive skill set.

But consider the countless other chances you have to push your daughter outside of her comfort zone and, in the process, help her prepare for and manage the uneasiness that comes with new people, new environments, and new experiences. So she can

Her Ability to Adapt Will Be Key

practise, from a young age, dealing with the emotional and behavioural demands of being adaptable. Perhaps it's about what after-school activity she chooses, what service outing she'll participate in with your church, synagogue, or mosque, or which classmates she picks for a special project in school. Or maybe it's when she has the chance to go to overnight camp or join a travelling sports team. For teachers, it might be about the class trip to a culturally unique part of town or how a student engages in open-ended hands-on projects. Take a moment before and after whatever boundary-breaking moment your girl is facing to candidly discuss how she felt, how she handled things, and what would help the next time she's facing similar uncertainty head-on. Together, you can reflect on what actions and ways of thinking most helped her adjust to the changing circumstances and manage feelings of uneasiness along the way.

At these times, also resist the natural tendency to smooth your daughter's way too much. When choosing a summer camp or service programme, pause before selecting the one that all of your daughter's schoolmates attend. When mulling over what class you request she's in for the coming year, think twice before defaulting to the teacher she's most familiar with or the class with all her friends. For that class project, avoid letting the students automatically resort to the same pairs or teams they're used to. Maybe the alternate option, the one that would push your girl to get to know new people in a different setting, would be a great chance to build her confidence in her adaptive skills. And show her how rewarding it can be to dive headfirst into uncertainty.

What Girls Need

For Chloe, the cheerful middle schooler we talked about in Chapter 3, this strategy made a lasting impact. She spent most of her childhood in the same house and the same neighbourhood, and even went to a primary school where her dad worked. At some point her parents consciously started pushing Chloe outside her comfort zone by having her spend more and more time with new people in new environments. In particular, when Chloe turned ten, her mum decided it was time for overnight camp—and not just any camp, but one in the distant woods of northern Maine, where the sense of security that came from summers spent at a ballet class with lifelong friends and playing in the garden with neighbours would be swapped for canoeing, camping, and other unfamiliar activities with girls she'd never met.

Three years later, when Chloe talks about her weeks in the woods, her smile and the pace at which she tells her story are telltale signs—not just about how much fun she had at camp and how happy she was to make new friends, but also of the confidence she gained in her capacity to respond to change and adjust to new situations as they arise.

Chloe's mum agrees. "Looking back on it, those few weeks at summer camp helped more than I realized," she says. "It was Chloe's biggest advantage when we had to abruptly move last year and she had to join a new school, make new friends, and deal with so much uncertainty . . . in the middle of middle school, too.

"She was still nervous those first few days in a strange school. But she knew that she could handle the change. That confidence made all the difference."

Alongside intentionally helping our girls practise being

Her Ability to Adapt Will Be Key

comfortable with everyday moments of discomfort, we must also build up our girls' ability to handle failure and help them internalize the notion that responding to uncertainty means taking risks, making mistakes, and bouncing back from disappointment and failure. As any parent, grandparent, teacher, or mentor of a young woman knows, this is particularly critical for today's girls, who often hold fast to a destructive sense of perfectionism through their teenage years and beyond. But given the multitude of studies, articles online, and books written on the subject of growth mindset and resilience, you may find yourself overwhelmed by the goal of helping our girls deal with real or perceived failures and rebound quickly in the face of adversity. In the context of developing adaptability, how can we put this idea into action, in a parent- and kid-friendly way? What does this look like for you and your girl?

One of the best strategies here is to use one-on-one moments with your daughter to be a little more vulnerable and honest, with yourself and your girl, as you speak about dealing with change and uncertainty in your own life. Research shows that storytelling helps improve adaptive performance, but that the lesson sinks in better when we hear about other people's mistakes rather than about their stories of success. So when you talk to your girl about times you tried to adapt to the world around you, share moments of failure—those times when you worked through major or minor transitions and navigated ambiguity but it didn't go as you had hoped or intended. For example, consider what personal anecdote to tell your daughter as you help her get ready for her first day at school or pack for her first time at overnight camp.

What Girls Need

This might be the right time to share that you were anxious the first nights you slept away from home and maybe reveal something that went wrong those few weeks you were away—not to scare her, but to talk through what you did that helped, what you could've done differently, and how things worked out in the end. We need to make sure our girls understand that their ability to handle the changes that life brings goes hand in hand with mistakes, missteps, and moments of failure.

Another strategy that parents find useful—and manageable—is to establish a routine that makes this sort of storytelling both easy and natural for the entire family. Kara, the middle school assembly speaker we heard from earlier, thinks such a routine empowers her to manage the disappointment and negative feelings that come with making mistakes. Her parents call this their "highs and lows", though I've heard others call it their "blips and dips" or "roses and thorns". Every day, at dinner or on the car ride home from ice-skating practice, her mum recounts a favourite moment from the day and something that didn't go quite right. Then Kara and her two siblings do the same. They talk about anything and everything, from a good (or poor) performance on a test to the moment Kara fell at a big skating competition or the feeling she had when her dog greeted her at the door. Her parents' goal is to normalize the candid discussion of mistakes, without judgement, and to remind the kids that there is always something to balance any real or perceived failure.

"It takes three minutes. Maybe ten," explains Kara. "But it reinforces that your day is never all bad. Even if your high might seem tiny... Like finding a penny in my bag."

Her Ability to Adapt Will Be Key

How does this help with ambiguity? you might wonder. Kara answers that question before I even have the chance to ask it. "It's the same with change," she says. "There will always be something good."

A final critical piece to keep front of mind in this push for adaptability is how we nurture our girls' love of learning, particularly in their preteen and early teenage years, when children learn not just *what* to learn but *how* to learn, too. And when many kids lose their natural excitement for traditional forms of education, as primary school "fun" is replaced by the stresses of life in middle and secondary school. This makes the late primary and middle school years a valuable period to foster our daughters' passion for learning (and relearning) new skills or ways of thinking. In the process, you'll help ensure she's prepared to grab new opportunities as she gets older and ready to continually reinvent herself to thrive in a certainly uncertain future.

But what does "encourage a love of learning" look like in the chaos of everyday life? As with many of the skills and behaviours we've discussed in this book, the answer lies in taking small, age-appropriate steps personalized for your girl. More specifically, it means using manageable strategies to nurture her curiosity about whatever piques her interest on a given day, and helping her apply that inquisitiveness not just at school but to the world around her. Watch for opportunities to help your girl embrace moments of natural real-world learning, no matter how messy—literally and figuratively—they may seem. Jennifer, a parent of two teenage girls, grabbed one such opportunity when she encouraged her younger daughter's love of making cupcakes.

What Girls Need

What started out as a way to distract then eleven-year-old Abby during a snow day with a box of Duncan Hines cake mix quickly became an at-home version of the TV show *Cupcake Wars*. Jennifer noticed that her girl's inquisitiveness was sparked by the process of baking, saw her competitive spirit fuelled by the desire to make the best cupcakes in the neighbourhood, and appreciated her daughter's desire to test the chemistry behind a favourite dessert by trying out different ingredients in different proportions. So she replaced Abby's cake mix with bags of flour, sugar, and other basic ingredients, and left her to a hands-on exploration of the art and science behind baking in her free time.

Upon reflection a few years later, Jennifer admits that she was amazed to see her daughter's excitement about such an everyday, seemingly trivial activity. And those hours in the kitchen had more impact than she realized at the time. Indeed, Abby still continues to invent new recipes that test her baking skills and quietly dreams of being a famous baker when she's older. As important, every time Jennifer brought home another bag of flour from the market, she reinforced her daughter's love of learning. Her girl's "aha" moment was not one single event but a serious of short, often messy, bursts of insight and discovery. Setting Abby free in the kitchen was an ideal personalized way to help her revel in the easy fun that accompanies real-world learning.

On a daily basis, this translates into simply playing the role of attentive observer of, facilitator for, and cheerleader for your girl's personal passions—whatever she finds interesting at a particular age or stage, whether that's dinosaurs or princesses, computer science or art, something big and flashy or something small and off the beaten path. As an attentive observer, you want to watch out for what brings your daughter joy and validate it as a serious interest, worthy of her attention. As a facilitator for her love of learning, ask open-ended questions that help her think creatively about whatever is on her mind and that naturally lead to further exploration. Questions that start with "how" and "why" are most helpful here, because they trigger not just reflection but curiosity, too. Then consider giving your daughter extra time on the computer or phone to find the answer. Or find some books and magazines, online videos, or museum exhibitions that focus on her interest. As a cheerleader for her love of learning, try to find and build excitement in the little discoveries—and, likely, little mistakes—that she makes along the way. Perhaps you can even set aside time at dinner or the next family gathering for her to tell everyone about what she's learned.

By highlighting the joy inherent in discovering new things, you'll help her recapture that feeling again and again. In the process, you will feed your daughter's appetite for learning and ensure that she develops into an agile thinker and avid learner. This will help make adaptability her competitive advantage for years to come.

As our military convoy bounced down the uneven road, my Kevlar helmet kept falling every which way. With one hand, I pulled my ponytail lower, hoping it would stop bumping against the back of my helmet every time we hit a hole in the roughly paved highway. My other hand was so firmly wrapped around my safety harness that its strap was cutting into my palm. But the dull pain was better than knocking into the soldier next to me—a young infantryman who was serving as our gunner, standing in the armoured vehicle's open turret with his weapon at the ready and scanning the area around us for suicide bombers, improvised explosive devices (IEDs), and other common threats.

We were an hour into what should've been a four-hour drive through the mostly barren land from a forward operating base in Qalat, capital of the southeastern Afghan province of Zabul, to the Kandahar air base, home to U.S. and international military forces in southern Afghanistan. Unfortunately, the trip was going to take much longer than usual.

The convoy of Mine-Resistant Ambush-Protected (MRAP) vehicles was hastily scheduled after our small base had been attacked the day prior. A suicide bomber's explosives had detonated on the road beside the thick security wall surrounding the military installation, which was home to a few hundred American soldiers and civilians working to support the local government and Afghan residents. Unfortunately, the only victims were two Afghan children who'd been playing in the street. One young boy had been airlifted to Kandahar, to receive medical treatment at the military hospital there. We were now transporting the child's father to his bedside.

Considering the previous day's attack, recent heightened concern about roadside bombs in the local area, and the fact that our five-vehicle convoy was crossing an area of Afghanistan considered a stronghold for the Taliban and Al-Qaeda, we stopped and started more than usual. Each time, soldiers would jump from the relative safety of our armoured vehicles and walk along the road's rocky edge, trying to spot explosives before they detonated.

Still, our sweltering MRAP was filled with the jovial banter typical of any long road trip with friends. Bad jokes and playful insults filled the armoured vehicle's crackling intercom. The soldiers I was with had been passing time on risky convoys through one of the poorest, least developed, and most volatile regions of Afghanistan for many months. It was new to me, having only recently arrived in Kandahar, but these guys had been through it before.

I craned my neck to look through the metal slats that covered the MRAP's small windows, hoping to get a better sense of what had stopped our forward progress that time. As I caught sight of two soldiers scanning the brush to our convoy's right, looking for the wires that indicate a nearby improvised explosive device, I unconsciously reached for the small bag at my feet. I was checking for the notebooks inside, which were filled with hundreds of pages of notes from my past two weeks of research in southern Afghanistan.

Scrawled in the small black books were handwritten transcripts of my interviews with former Taliban and tribal elders, Afghan prisoners and their family members, Zabul's provincial governor and his staff, plus members of the local peace council, who were coordinating "Afghan Peace and Reintegration Efforts" in the region. Some pages held messy hand-drawn diagrams of the secure facilities I'd visited, or hastily jotted-down emails and phone numbers for the local Afghans I'd met who wanted to stay in touch. And there were dozens of candid quotes and revealing stories from soldiers, Taliban fighters, and government officials I interviewed, who wanted to provide input into my work on peace and reconciliation efforts in Afghanistan. They included input from Hameed, the young Afghan I'd met the day prior, who'd wistfully observed that "in our culture, when people want peace, they stop war. But you keep fighting, even though you want peace."

In other words, the notebooks contained insights I wanted to keep safe, no matter what else happened.

As I watched the soldiers outside my window make their way back to the armoured vehicle, confident for the moment that our convoy was safe to proceed, I pulled two of the books from my backpack and shoved them between my flak jacket and my chest. I held them there for the next six hours, until we reached the relative safety of Kandahar air base.

I couldn't do much to address the uncertainty, discomfort, and uneasiness of that day, but at least I could protect the answers I already had with me.

I used to hate uncertainty," Kara concludes, as she finishes explaining why imagining life as an adult made her worry about control and stability. "I hated moving. I hated when a relative moved. I hated when a project changed.

"Now I'm getting pretty good at adapting," she admits sheepishly. "I'm working on it."

"What helped?" I ask.

"Well..."

Her Ability to Adapt Will Be Key

I watch as Kara crosses and uncrosses her legs, twisting her hands around her knees as she searches her mind for the right answer. I didn't fully realize the power of adaptability until I was an adult, so I'm eager to hear a middle schooler explain her personal path to adaptable proficiency.

"I've moved seven times. I've switched to a lot of different schools," Kara says. "That's a lot of houses. A lot of friends. A lot of skating rinks. I've had so much change that I got used to it. I know it always gets better.

"That's probably extreme," she continues, no doubt catching my look of surprise when she described moving seven times before finishing Year 9. "But you have to make sure that if something goes wrong, you can change."

Kara breaks into a broad smile, as if suddenly realizing the advantage that adaptability provides her—not just during moves, in a skating competition, or at a new school, but throughout life.

"Looking at the exciting things in the future helped me not worry about the changes in the present. When I'm older, I think I'll use that strategy, too."

I can't wait to see Kara and her friends in action in the years to come. They will no doubt face life's certain uncertainty with not just confidence and resilience but also with a practised ability to embrace ambiguity and change.

Conclusion

Why It Matters,
Take Two

I pull the top off the large cardboard box, lugged from the back of a closet where it had sat, untouched, since we moved three years earlier. It will take more than a few minutes to rifle through its contents, so I unceremoniously plop onto the floor of our guest room/office/extra stuff room to take a closer look.

Within seconds, I forget about the mess around me—work dresses tossed on the bed waiting to go to the dry cleaners, out-of-season clothes collecting dust on a corner chair, and a pile of folded decorative gift bags ready to be reused on a yet-to-be-determined present. Also forgotten are work emails demanding an answer, texts from friends needing a response, and voice mails from my mother, who still hasn't quite mastered texting.

My attention is quickly consumed by what's inside the non-descript box. I rediscover fifteen neatly stacked notebooks, labelled to identify what country or combat zone I'd carried them in and what stories they held. There are also folders with itineraries from trips to Kabul, receipts from the hotel in Riyadh that I called home for a bit too long, and a pile of tattered business cards from government officials around the world who'd given off-the-record advice. I also find a colourful picture that a ten-year-old Yemeni girl drew for me when I joined her family for lunch at their home in Sana'a.

I open the top notebook to a random page and instantly am transported from the Philadelphia suburbs to the hard, dirty floor of a converted metal shipping container that is home to a Syrian family in Jordan's Zaatari refugee camp. Mats tucked in the corner are pulled out each night to serve as beds for the family's three children. A boxy television silently plays a Turkish soap opera, throwing odd colours around the dimly lit room. On my right sits a young girl. She scooches up next to me as I interview her mother and father, curious about who I am and what is in my oversize satchel. I reach inside the bag to grab my phone and distract her with pictures of my cat as I talk with her parents, whose story of fleeing from Aleppo to this refugee camp along the Jordan–Syrian border was a poignant lesson in self-advocacy, resilience, and adaptability.

A few years later, I scan my notes from that day and remember details of the story that I hoped to share in this book. So that lessons I learned during my time in the field could help not just the girls at my school but other young women and the parents, teachers, and adults cheering them on. I suddenly think of Brianna, the student I spoke about in the introduction who had seen real-world gender bias play out with her teenage friends in ways new to her but familiar to every working woman I know. I recall the story she shared about how she found her voice.

"When I was in middle school, I started to write poetry," Brianna once told me during a mentorship session. "I always loved making up stories and writing poems. I didn't think I was particularly good at it, but I still liked it a lot.

"I can remember my dad telling me that my poems were really good, that they were worth sharing. I always thought he was such a good writer, so when he complimented me ..." Brianna shrugged, her words trailing off like the untied shoelaces on her sneakers.

"I thought I must be kind of good at it, too," she concluded. "It gave me confidence in my own voice."

Before I can mentally dust off more details from Brianna's story, the high-pitched wails of an infant tug me back to reality. My six-week-old baby boy in his bassinet wants to be fed.

I pull myself off the floor with a sigh, switching back into mum mode. I try to remember when the baby last ate and wonder—aloud but mostly to myself—when the feeding schedule our paediatrician recommended will start to work.

A few minutes later, as I settle into the couch and watch my newborn contentedly sucking a bottle, my mind wanders to all the ingredients in this book—anecdotes from corporate leaders and military officers, stories from students and parents, and academic research from psychologists, economists, and even zoologists. In the few minutes of welcome silence that follow, as the baby falls asleep, I start to think about how much all of these lessons matter—not just for school-aged girls worried about the world awaiting them, parents eager to prepare their daughters for whatever challenge they'll face in the future, and teachers searching for better ways to empower young women with the strength of their natural advantages. But also for me, now more than ever.

Revisiting the "game face" lesson I learned at flight school, I see how that strategy still helps me lean into daily challenges and inspires me to employ a healthy competitive spirit to my advantage. I suddenly remember the moments when community members openly questioned my plan to return to work six weeks after giving birth, on a schedule that felt best for my family and me. My game face mattered then as much as ever. It helped me tap into my self-confidence, trust that I'd be able to adapt to the major life changes ahead, and speak out in a way that felt right to me. The ability to reframe the challenges ahead as a competition provided me with a distinct set of strategic skills, so I could embrace the sort of assertive attitude that steadied me in the face of public judgement.

Research on how to help girls effectively ask likewise took on additional meaning after my child was born. It gave me the confidence to ask my school's board, who collectively serve as my boss, to accommodate my maternity leave by rescheduling an important quarterly meeting so that I could meet the needs of the baby and my job, which both matter to me a great deal. The ability to ask empowered me in tricky conversations with my husband about how I wanted us to share responsibilities as new parents. I could let him know with confidence what I needed as a mother, what support I wanted when I returned to work, and what I craved most as I defined myself in a new way.

Rereading studies on collaborative problem-solving and empathy, I think again about that first week after we brought the baby home. Our little boy developed jaundice and lost a lot of weight, complications common in newborns. My husband and I ended up in the Accident and Emergency unit with our four-day-old, a development that neither of us could deal with on our own. We needed the help of a team of doctors, lactation consultants, friends, family, and more—a network of support that helped the baby and me get through those difficult early days.

The ability to be adaptable also became more important after my baby was born, given the jarring uncertainty and sense of WTF that now consumed nearly every minute of my day and many nights, too. The practice I had managing the unknown and adjusting to massive personal and professional change helped me adapt emotionally, mentally, and physically to a new schedule, a new imbalance, and a new me. It enabled me to weather the ups and downs that accompany major life milestones, and that felt especially acute after giving birth.

As my career unfolded, I'd started to appreciate how all of these skills and ways of being were essential to my success. My daily life as a parent then revealed how these specific tools empower me in more ways than I ever realized. Understanding the strength of my voice, competitive spirit, persuasiveness, and adaptability helps me be a better version of myself, as a woman, a leader, and a mum. In my current role as the head of an all-girls school, I watch our students, teachers, and parents in action and see how much today's girls need these lessons, too.

With all of this in mind, I recently reached out to Brianna for an update on life since graduation. She is now at college, dealing with all the typical challenges that come with leaving home, navigating different social dynamics and new academic demands, and figuring out how to "adult". Like many kids her age, Brianna wants to be a tech entrepreneur, though she also admits that it's intimidating to see how few women and people of colour have found success in this space. As we discuss how she might tackle these common real-world obstacles, the nineteen-year-old stops to reminisce about what helped most when she was young.

"I realize now how much I observed everything around me," she says. "Every comment I heard, or thing I saw. Even when my parents thought no one was watching. Young girls internalize everything. We're sponges."

I ask what that means for adults with a special girl or young woman in their life.

"No one has to be perfect," she continues. "But parents or teachers or older siblings play a huge role. The little things we do to empower girls are so important, particularly when they come from someone a girl looks up to... It's not just about how women speak about ourselves and what we're capable of. It's how we help girls take that on."

No matter how much progress we make addressing the gender-based inequities and discrimination that remain pervasive in the modern workplace and wider world, our daughters will face specific gender-based challenges for decades to come.

Why It Matters, Take Two

Giving our girls what they need early on is as important as ever, especially as they grow up in the twenty-first century, when new skills and ways of being will be more and more essential to success. Their natural talents for competing, collaboratively solving problems, leading with empathy, and adapting will make the biggest difference and be their greatest advantage—at home and work, as leaders and caregivers, and during the inner dialogue that we all have during periods of self-reflection.

That is why the little moments we take to empower our girls, when they're young, matter so much.

These days, when I see students in the halls or on the sidelines of a game, everyone asks about the baby. After I show them a recent picture on my phone, I remind them how much I count on support from the entire school community to help solve the usual problems that face any new mum. I mention how I've had to adapt not just my schedule and daily priorities, but my sense of self. And I talk about a difficult ask that I had to make of a colleague, friend, or family member. The lesson I want these girls to hear is "You can do this, too." In these brief moments, I want these girls to see that these important skills and ways of being are all within our—and their—reach.

Little things do make a big difference, to all of us and our girls.

Acknowledgements

If this book had one more chapter, it would describe the team that every girl needs to succeed. There would be a section on the impact of family members who serve as your loudest cheerleaders no matter what the scoreboard says, and on colleagues who become trusted confidants during life's many ups and downs. A portion would be devoted to the importance of mentors who challenge you even when it's easier to let things slide, and to friends who always take your calls to simply hear what's on your mind without judgement or offering solutions. The chapter would be filled with stories from the community of supporters on whom I have relied over many years for convoy rides, coffee breaks, moral support, career coaching, life advice, and more. But I'll save those fun and funny tidbits for the next book. Instead, I hope that this attempt to acknowledge the many people who influence my work makes clear the lasting impact of having a team by your side.

First, my tremendous thanks to the dynamic pair who made *What Girls Need* a reality. To my agent, Jim Levine, for your commitment to this book's message and your belief that its stories matter now more than ever. Thank you for your perceptive editorial input, sound advice, good humour, and endless expertise as you guided me at every step. I couldn't have asked for more. It was likewise a tremendous pleasure to work with Laura Tisdel, my masterful editor. Your care and attention to each word and every idea elevated not just my writing but my thinking, too. And your endless support during weeks of personal and professional craziness made me smile and breathe easier. I will be forever grateful to have you both on my team.

I'm also grateful for the support each of your teams provided throughout

Acknowledgements

this process. To Jim's crew, including Lindsay Edgecombe, Danielle Svetcov, and Monika Verma, thank you for your feedback on the proposal and manuscript, your patience (and endless follow-up emails) throughout, and your dedication to making this book a success. I was also fortunate to benefit from the entire Viking team's expertise, creativity, and enthusiasm for this book's message—especially Carolyn Coleburn and Linsday Prevette for publicity, Nicole Celli for production editing, Lynn Buckley for cover design, and Amanda Dewey for interior design.

To the many folks who believed in and supported *What Girls Need* from its inception, I will always appreciate the impact you had on the book itself and, I hope, on any young girl who will be bolder, more courageous, and more resilient because of its lessons. To Anne Plutzer, for years of creative brainstorming and always understanding what a friend needs most, including baby-holding at just the right time. To Genevieve and Genna Marvin, for helping shape the ideas in each chapter before there were even words on a page. To Abi Linnington, for openly sharing and personally modelling your lessons of leadership, motherhood, and service. To Sara Scott, for pushing me to share my story and, when it finally came together, generously opening doors for key interviews. To Ricki Weisberg Ndege, for knowing when to check in and how to push an old friend to share in a new, more vulnerable way. To Adam and Allison Grant, for advocating for this book as soon as its premise came up over dinner one night and for all your advice along the way. To Julia Maenza, my research assistant, for your above-and-beyond work on this project and your oh-so-Baldwin approach to getting things done, wherever you were in the world. I couldn't ask for a better team during the writing process.

This project also benefited considerably from the many friends, colleagues, and mentors whose wisdom and experience helped this book come to life and, as important, who always answer the phone no matter what else is happening. This group also includes the leading women and men who gave interviews or provided introductions for interviews for *What Girls Need*. Thank you to Patricia Ajoy, Elizabeth Arend, Margie Cohn, Jenny Cross, Adrienne Harris, Kate Hermsdorfer, Julissa Marenco, Jessica Meir, Paul Mrockowski, John Nagl, Dick Nodell, Martha Ortiz, Sejita Page, Courtney

Acknowledgements

Palaski, Steve Piltch, Mario Ramirez, Sarah Redmond, Sarah Robb O'Hagan, Rich Schellhas, Kate Shattuck, Melanie Sheerr, Gwen Shen, Amy Sobel, Rachel Stern, Pat Weiser, Jay Wiley, and Margie Yang. My sincere appreciation also to those who gave me opportunities and guidance throughout my career and who influenced the trajectory of my personal story, including Ajay Banga, Reuben Brigety, Richard Danzig, Harry Harris, Rich Hooker, Alan Liotta, H.R. McMaster, Tom Monheim, Jim Stavridis, and Mary and Jeff Zients. I hope every girl is fortunate enough to have such an exemplary group to serve as not just mentors but sponsors, too.

I could not be more grateful to the Baldwin School community, whose commitment to giving every girl what she needs was the driving force behind this book. Watching Baldwin's faculty and staff in action and remembering my own Baldwin teachers compelled me to write these chapters. Connecting with alumnae motivated me to find better ways to tell these stories. Working with fellow administrators—including Laura Blankenship, Cindy Lapinski, Elizabeth Becker, Anne Longley, Meg Glascott-Birch, Quenby Frimet, and Tejan Walcott—provided the book's best ideas. Baldwin's board provided the support I needed to take on this project, and I'm especially grateful to Chris Marr and Terry Steelman for their leadership in that group's important work. Baldwin students not only supplied inspiring and funny anecdotes, but also motivated me to complete this project. I will be forever grateful to represent all of you in my current role and in this book, but most of all as a Baldwin alumna.

Finally, I want to share heartfelt thanks to my family for giving me what I needed to discover the lessons woven throughout this book. To Mom and Dad, your endless encouragement is what every daughter needs. To Stef and Jerry, Jen and Joe, Greg and Dianna, your steadfast support is what every little sister needs. Most of all, to my husband, without whom neither this book nor my work leading the next generation of Baldwin girls would be possible—Scott, thank you for being the bear to my badger. You make me a better writer and better thinker, a better leader and better friend, a better mom and better person. Isaac and I are lucky to have you.

Recommended Reading

What Girls Need is intended to jump-start the conversation about how we prepare today's young girls to succeed in the twenty-first-(and twenty-second-!) century world that awaits them. The below list of recommended further reading is intended to give parents, educators, and anyone with a school-aged girl in their life a few more resources on the topics raised in this book. Consider it a short list of other places you can turn to for additional ideas on how to raise bold, courageous, and resilient women.

If you're interested in reading more about the gender dynamics that influence our daughters (and sons), when they're young and as well as adults, check out:

- *Invisible Women: Exposing Data Bias in a World Designed for Men*, by Caroline Criado Perez (New York: Abrams, 2019). This well-researched and sharply written book details how gendered thinking creates persistent, systemic barriers for women around the world. Full of countless examples that will challenge your thinking about real-world data bias, it's a provocative way to think about how established gender inequities still impact our girls' lives on a daily basis.

- *What Works: Gender Equality by Design*, by Iris Bohnet (Cambridge: Belknap Press, 2016). Eager for more about what we can do to tackle institutional gender inequality? This book looks at data-driven ways to change systems that continue to hold women back. The author, a behavioural economist, uses social science research to suggest how we can influence human behaviour to counter unconscious gender bias in organizations.

- *The Athena Doctrine: How Women (and the Men Who Think Like Them) Will Rule the Future,* by John Gerzema and Michael D'Antonio (San Francisco: Jossey-Bass, 2013). This book is for anyone inspired by—or curious about—the idea that the "future is female". Using surveys and stories from around the world, the authors examine why traits typically considered "feminine" are increasingly critical to successful leadership. It also provides an insightful way to take a closer look at one's own leadership style.

- *What Works for Women at Work: Four Patterns Working Women Need to Know,* by Joan Williams and Rachel Dempsey (New York: New York University Press, 2014). Looking for a how-to guide to address common patterns of workplace gender bias? This book combines scientific research and interviews with women at different stages of their careers to identify four types of biased behaviour that hamper women professionally. While not intended for parents per se, it gives a helpful perspective on the challenges awaiting our girls and practical advice for anyone working outside the home.

If you want additional strategies and actionable steps to help prepare your girl to thrive when she's older, personally and professionally, try:

- *UnSelfie: Why Empathetic Kids Succeed in Our All-About-Me World,* by Michele Borba (New York: Touchstone, 2016). If you were particularly inspired by the discussion of empathy, this book is for you. The author explores why it's so important to teach today's kids about empathetic thinking and outlines every-day strategies that parents can use to help school-aged children understand and practise empathy on a daily basis.

- *The Gift of Failure: How The Best Parents Learn To Let Go So Their Children Can Succeed,* by Jessica Lahey (New York:

Recommended Reading

Harper, 2015). Given the perfectionist tendencies of many preteen and teenage girls, this book is a great source for ideas on improving your daughter's ability to handle failure and, thus, nurturing her adaptability. The author shares practical advice and heartwarming stories about how adults can help children learn from setbacks and become more resilient, adaptable, and ready for the real world.

- *How to Raise Successful People: Simple Lessons for Radical Results*, by Esther Wojcicki (Boston: Houghton Mifflin Harcourt, 2019). Drawing from her decades as a classroom teacher and mother of three women who became superstars in traditionally male-dominated industries, the author provides easily digestible philosophies for modern parenting. It also underscores the important lesson that, when it comes to empowering kids to be their best selves, little things have a big impact.

- *Prepared: What Kids Needs for a Fulfilled Life*, by Diane Tavenner (New York: Currency, 2019). If you want another inspiring parenting reference, try this book. Based on the author's experience leading a network of innovative charter schools, it provides tangible advice for nurturing kids' curiosity and independent growth. The author also investigates what universal skills kids need to be successful adults and reminds us why it's critical to nurture girls' love of learning from a young age.

- *Under Pressure: Confronting the Epidemic of Stress and Anxiety in Girls* (New York: Ballantine, 2019) and *Untangled: Guiding Teenage Girls Through the Seven Transitions into Adulthood* (New York: Ballantine, 2016), both by Lisa Damour. No conversation about raising girls is complete without considering the social and emotional stressors facing our girls, particularly as they navigate challenging developmental stages of their teenage years. These two books use social science and neuroscience research alongside lessons from the author's work as a clinical psychotherapist to describe how parents and educators can support girls through common social-emotional challenges that many young women encounter.

- *Girls & Sex: Navigating the Complicated New Landscape* (New York: HarperCollins, 2016), by Peggy Orenstein. Parents of teens or preteens no doubt also have questions about how modern views on sex and sexuality influence our girls. This book is a thought-provoking look at those complicated subjects as seen and experienced by girls today. It thus serves as a helpful resource on how to encourage healthy discussions about sex, relationships, consent, and more with your daughter.

If you'd like to explore further debates about the future of work and the sorts of challenges and opportunities that our children will face when they're adults, consider:

- *21 Lessons for the 21st Century*, Yuval Noah Harari (New York: Spiegel & Grau, 2018). Want to know more about how educators, business executives, world leaders, and more picture our certainly uncertain future? Harari's book is a thought-provoking and easy-to-read survey of major social, technological, and ideological shifts that will likely impact the next decade and beyond. It will challenge your thinking about how we should prepare children now for what might await them as adults in the twenty-first (and twenty-second) century.

- *The Inevitable: Understanding the 12 Technological Forces That Will Shape Our Future*, by Kevin Kelly (New York: Viking, 2016). Technological developments will no doubt significantly impact what life looks like when today's young girls are adults. This book provides an engaging way to think about how major technological trends will drive cultural change over the next thirty years, providing additional context for any discussion about what our kids need to succeed personally and professionally.

Notes

Author's Note: What Girls Need

xiv **23 per cent of young women:** "Sexual Assault Statistics." National Sexual Violence Resource Center; https://www.nsvrc.org/node/4737.

xiv **42 per cent of women:** Kim Parker and Cary Funk, "Gender Discrimination Comes in Many Forms for Today's Working Women." *Fact Tank,* Pew Research Center, pewresearch.org, December 14, 2017.

Introduction: Challenges and Opportunities Awaiting Our Girls

4 **77 per cent of teachers:** Richard M. Ingersoll, Elizabeth Merrill, Daniel Stuckey, and Gregory Collins, "Seven Trends: The Transformation of the Teaching Force." *CPRE Research Reports,* October 2018, 13.

4 **two-thirds of private school heads:** "Female Heads 'Under-Represented in Secondary Schools,' Says Study." BBC, April 7, 2017.

5 **"negative association with academic rank":** "More Needs to Be Done to Address the Gender Gap in Academia, Researchers Say." Cardiff University, *Phys.org,* June 6, 2019.

5 **under a quarter of the seats:** Drew DeSilver, "A Record Number of Women Will Be Serving in the New Congress." Pew Research Center, December 18, 2018.

5 **greater than 50 per cent:** "Gender Distribution of the Resident Population of the United States from 1980 to 2018." *Statista,* 2018.

5 **few countries come anywhere close:** "Female Share of Seats in National Parliaments." *OECD.*

Notes

6 **4.2 per cent since 2001:** Figure derived from U.S. Census Bureau reports.

6 **moving from 2059 to 2119:** Kevin Miller and Deborah J. Vagins, "The Simple Truth About the Gender Pay Gap." AAUW, Spring 2018, 5; Amy Becker, "Gender Pay Gap Remains at 20 Cents." *AAUW,* September 12, 2017.

6 **efforts stalled:** Henrik Kleven, Camille Landais, and Jakob Egholt Søgaard, "Children and Gender Inequality: Evidence from Denmark." *NBER Working Paper No. 24219,* January 2018.

6 **motherhood penalty can even impede the career progress:** Safia Samee Ali, "'Motherhood Penalty' Can Affect Women Who Never Even Have a Child." NBC News, April 11, 2016; Natalie Kitroeff and Jessica Silver-Greenberg, "Pregnancy Discrimination Is Rampant Inside America's Biggest Companies." *New York Times,* February 8, 2019.

7 **all but one was a man:** Noam Scheiber and John Eligon, "Elite Law Firm's All-White Partner Class Stirs Debate on Diversity." *New York Times,* January 27, 2019.

7 **"ramble and miss the point":** Emily Peck, "Women at Ernst & Young Instructed on How to Dress, Act Nicely Around Men." *HuffPost,* October 21, 2019.

7 **receptionist was sent home:** Dan Bilefsky, "Sent Home for Not Wearing Heels, She Ignited a British Rebellion." *New York Times,* January 25, 2017.

8 **"born a girl":** Bill Gates and Melinda Gates, "Examining Inequality." Gates Foundation, 2019; https://www.gatesfoundation.org/goal keepers/report/2019-report/#ExaminingInequality.

11 **"defining economic feature of our era":** Lawrence H. Summers, "Economic Possibilities for Our Children." NBER Reporter, 2013, No. 4; https://www.nber.org/reporter/2013number4/2013no4.pdf.

12 **65 per cent of kids:** "The Future of Jobs Report." World Economic Forum, January 2016; http://www3.weforum.org/docs/WEF_Future _of_Jobs.pdf.

12 **133 million new jobs:** Oliver Cann, "Machines Will Do More Tasks Than Humans by 2025 but Robot Revolution Will Still Create 58

Notes

Million Net New Jobs in Next Five Years." World Economic Forum, September 17, 2018; https://www.weforum.org/press/2018/09/machines-will-do-more-tasks-than-humans-by-2025-but-robot-revolution-will-still-create-58-million-net-new-jobs-in-next-five-years/.

12 **interacting with different cultures:** "Preparing Our Youth for an Inclusive and Sustainable World: The OECD PISA Global Competence Framework 2018." OECD, 2018; https://www.oecd.org/education/Global-competency-for-an-inclusive-world.pdf.

13 **Today's students must be taught:** J. Phillip Schmidt, Mitchel Resnick, and Joi Ito, "Creative Learning and the Future of Work", in *Disrupting Unemployment*, ed. Max Senges et al. (Kansas City, MO: IIIJ Foundation, 2016).

13 **tackle challenges in multidisciplinary ways:** Karri Holley, "Interdisciplinary Curriculum and Learning in Higher Education." *Oxford Research Encyclopedia of Education,* April 2017; DOI: https://dx.doi.org/10.1093/acrefore/9780190264093.013.138.

Chapter 1. Help Her Find Her Voice

25 **20 per cent of female college students:** "The Criminal Justice System: Statistics," RAINN; https://www.rainn.org/statistics/criminal-justice-system.

25 **Three out of four people:** Chai R. Feldblum and Victoria A. Lipnic, "Select Task Force on the Study of Harassment in the Workplace." U.S. Equal Employment Opportunity Commission, June 2016, v; https://www.eeoc.gov/eeoc/task_force/harassment/report.cfm.

30 **amount you verbally participate in group discussions:** Victoria L. Brescoll, "Who Takes the Floor and Why: Gender, Power, and Volubility in Organizations." *Administrative Science Quarterly 56,* no. 4, (2011); R. F. Bales, *Interaction Process Analysis: A Method for the Study of Small Groups* (Cambridge, MA: Addison-Wesley, 1950).

30 **how much influence you have:** R. F. Bales, F. L. Strodtbeck, T. M. Mills, and M. E. Roseborough, "Channels of Communication in Small Groups." *American Sociological Review* 16, no. 4 (August 1951): 461–68.

Notes

30 "Being assertive is as important as anything": Personal conversations with Colonel Abigail Linnington, July 2019.

30 female college students are less likely: Alecia J. Carter et al., "Women's Visibility in Academic Seminars: Women Ask Fewer Questions Than Men." *PLoS One* 13, no. 9 (September 27, 2018); Sarah L. Eddy, Sara E. Brownell, and Mary Pat Wenderoth, "Gender Gaps in Achievement and Participation in Multiple Introductory Biology Classrooms." CBE—Life Sciences Education 13, no. 3 (September 2014).

31 women receive less credit: Heather Sarsons, "Gender Differences in Recognition for Group Work." *Working Paper,* December 3, 2015; https://scholar.harvard.edu/files/sarsons/files/gender_groupwork .pdf?m=1449178759; Madeline E. Heilman and Michelle C. Haynes, "No Credit Where Credit Is Due: Attributional Rationalization of Women's Success in Male-Female Teams." *Journal of Applied Psychology* 90, no. 5 (2005): 905–16.

31 because of speech patterns: Rindy C. Anderson et al., "Vocal Fry May Undermine the Success of Young Women in the Labor Market." *PLoS One* 9, no. 5 (2014).

31 70 per cent of all panel speakers: Shivina Kumar, "Almost 70% of Professional Event Speakers Are Male." *The Bizzabo Blog,* November 1, 2018.

31 number hovers around 80 per cent: Leila Fadel, "Survey Suggests 'Manels'—All-Male Panels—Are Still the Norm." *NPR,* November 1, 2018.

32 grassroots movements to address the imbalance: A number of examples can be found, across sectors, of community-based efforts to increase the number of women on professional panels, including Owen Barder, "The Pledge—I Will Not Be Part of Male-Only Panels", *Owen.org;* "Say No to #ManPanels", *ManPanels.org;* Virginia Gewin, "How the Creators of a Database Are Stamping Out All-Male Panels", *Nature,* May 10, 2019, https://www.nature.com /articles/d41586-019-01500-3.

32 make light of the situation: Michael Skapinker, "Ending Men-Only Panels Is a Spur to Creativity." *Financial Times,* April 23, 2018.

Notes

32 **impact of innovation on business:** Eric Schmidt, Megan Smith, and Walter Isaacson, "How Innovation Happens." YouTube video, filmed July 13, 2015, at SXSW in Austin, Texas.

33 **"Research tells us that women are interrupted":** Karissa Bell, "Google Chairman Gets Called Out for Cutting Off a Woman While Talking About Diversity." *Mashable,* March 16, 2015; Danny Yadron, "Thoughts on Gender Equality in Tech, Interrupted." *Wall Street Journal,* March 16, 2015.

33 **"you have interrupted Megan":** T. C. Sottek, "Google Executive Eric Schmidt, Man, Makes Total Ass of Himself at SXSW." *The Verge,* March 16, 2015.

34 **long-held perception that women speak more than men:** Deborah Tannen, "The Truth About How Much Women Talk—and Whether Men Listen." *Time,* June 28, 2017; Nikhil Swaminathan, "Gender Jabber: Do Women Talk More Than Men?" *Scientific American,* July 6, 2007. See also Matthias R. Mehl et al., "Are Women Really More Talkative Than Men?" *Science* 317, no. 5834 (August 2007).

34 **forty-six to two:** Don H. Zimmerman and Candace West, "Sex Roles, Interruptions and Silences in Conversation", in *Language and Sex: Difference and Dominance,* ed. Barrie Thorne and Nancy Henley (New York: Newbury House Publishers, 1975), 105–29.

35 **"different socialization patterns":** Deborah Tannen, *Talking from 9 to 5* (New York: William Morrow, 1994), 300.

35 **"penalized for speaking out":** Susan Chira, "The Universal Phenomenon of Men Interrupting Women." *New York Times,* June 14, 2017.

35 **65.9 per cent of all interruptions:** Tonja Jacobi and Dylan Schweers, "Justice, Interrupted: The Effect of Gender, Ideology and Seniority at Supreme Court Oral Arguments." *Virginia Law Review* 103, no. 1379 (2017): 1459.

36 **three female justices on the bench:** Tonja Jacobi and Dylan Schweers, "Female Supreme Court Justices Are Interrupted More by Male Justices and Advocates." *Harvard Business Review,* April 11, 2017.

Notes

36 **men gave over twice as many speeches:** Christine Nittrouer et al., "Gender Disparities in Colloquium Speakers at Top Universities." *PNAS* 115, no. 1 (January 2018), 106.

36 **gender disparity in Silicon Valley:** Kieran Snyder, "How to Get Ahead as a Woman in Tech: Interrupt Men." *Slate*, July 23, 2014.

36 **the medical field:** Candace West, "When the Doctor Is a 'Lady': Power, Status and Gender in Physician-Patient Encounters." *Symbolic Interaction* 7, no. 1 (Spring 1984): 87–106.

36 **local school boards:** Christopher F. Karpowitz and Tali Mendelberg, *The Silent Sex: Gender, Deliberation, and Institutions* (Princeton, NJ: Princeton University Press, 2014); Marie Tessier, "Speaking While Female, and at a Disadvantage." *New York Times*, October 27, 2016.

37 **28 per cent of participants:** Emma Pierson, "Outnumbered but Well-Spoken: Female Commenters in the New York Times", in *CSCW '15: Proceedings of the 18th ACM Conference on Computer Supported Cooperative Work & Social Computing*, 1201–13.

37 **study of girls and boys playing together:** Kieran Snyder, "Boys Learn to Interrupt. Girls Learn to Shut Up." *Slate*, August 14, 2014.

46 **soften our style of communication:** Tara Mohr, *Playing Big: Practical Wisdom for Women Who Want to Speak Up, Create, and Lead* (New York: Avery, 2015).

47 **framing questions with polite openings:** Jacobi and Schweers, "Female Supreme Court Justices."

47 **light-hearted approach to self-monitoring:** Jacobi and Schweers, "Female Supreme Court Justices."

Chapter 2. Turn Her Voice into an Influential Ask

53 **"not really about asking":** Selena Larson, "Microsoft CEO Satya Nadella to Women: Don't Ask for a Raise, Trust Karma." *ReadWrite*, October 9, 2014.

54 **"that's good karma":** Amit Chowdhry, "Microsoft CEO Satya Nadella Apologizes for Comments on Women's Pay." *Forbes*, October 10, 2014.

Notes

55 **workers change jobs more often:** Heather Long, "The New Normal: 4 Job Changes by the Time You're 32." *CNN Business,* April 12, 2016.

56 **women appear to job-hop more than men:** Alison Doyle, "How Often Do People Change Jobs During a Lifetime?" *The Balance Careers,* December 1, 2019; Guy Berger, "Will This Year's College Grads Job-Hop More Than Previous Grads?" LinkedIn, April 12, 2016.

56 **77 per cent of students:** Valerie J. Calderon, "U.S. Students' Entrepreneurial Energy Waiting to Be Tapped." Gallup, October 13, 2011.

56 **called entrepreneurial intention:** Julian E. Lange et al., "Global Entrepreneurship Monitor 2018/2019 United States Report." Babson College, 15; https://www.babson.edu/media/babson/assets/blank-center/GEM_USA_2018-2019.pdf.

56 **companies have started to alter:** Vinod Mohan, "Top 10 Talent Trends of 2019." *Korn Ferry Focus,* 2019.

57 **persuasive is essential for success:** First Round Review, "Let This Former Googler Help You Tap the Science of Persuasion." *Fast Company,* April 24, 2018.

57 **bottom of the wish list:** "Job Outlook 2019." National Association of Colleges and Employers, November 2018.

58 **children would impact their career:** "Time to Talk: What Has to Change for Women at Work." PwC, 2018; https://www.pwc.com/gx/en/about/diversity/internationalwomensday/time-to-talk-what-has-to-change-for-women-at-work.html.

58 **Forty-four per cent of professional women:** "Time to Talk: What Has to Change for Women at Work."

60 **"about German chancellor Angela Merkel's interest":** There were numerous reports by American and foreign press about Merkel's public statements on Guantánamo and the case of a particular detainee. See Richard Bernstein, "Merkel, on Visit, Will Try Gingerly to Revive U.S. Ties", *New York Times,* January 13, 2006; "Merkel fordert Schließung von Guantanamo", *Der Spiegel,* January 7, 2006; DW staff, "Germany Negotiates with US to Free Guantanamo Prisoner", *Deutsche Welle (DW),* February 6, 2006; https://www.dw.com/en/germany-negotiates-with-us-to-free-guantanamo-prisoner/a-1900697.

Notes

62 **"their own worst enemy":** Personal conversation with Julissa Marenco, January 3, 2019.

63 **advantage when buying a new car:** Ian Ayres and Peter Siegelman, "Race and Gender Discrimination in Bargaining for a New Car." *American Economic Review* 85, no. 3 (June 1995): 304–21.

65 **experiment to study how gender:** Meghan R. Busse, Florian Zettelmeyer, and Ayalet Israeli, "Repairing the Damage: The Effect of Price Knowledge and Gender on Auto-Repair Price Quotes." *Journal of Marketing Research* 54, no. 1 (2017): 75–95.

65 **$365 (£280) repair job:** The benchmark price of $365 was determined by AutoMD.com, an online search tool that helps users find local repair shops and determine how much common car problems should cost to fix.

66 **women's reluctance is a learned behaviour:** Sara Laschever, "Younger Women May Be Asking for Pay Rises. But Let's Not Celebrate Just Yet." The *Guardian*, September 9, 2016.

66 **57 per cent of the male graduate students:** Linda Babcock and Sara Laschever, *Women Don't Ask* (New York: Bantam, 2007); also Linda Babcock and Sara Laschever, *Ask for It* (New York: Bantam, 2009).

67 **only the woman was asked:** D. A. Small et al., "Who Goes to the Bargaining Table? The Influence of Gender and Framing on the Initiation of Negotiation." *Journal of Personality and Social Psychology* 93, no. 4 (2007): 600–13.

67 **other similar job listings:** Andreas Leibbrandt and John A. List, "Do Women Avoid Salary Negotiations? Evidence from a Large-Scale Natural Field Experiment." *Management Science* 61, no. 9 (2015): 2016–24.

68 **women negotiate online:** Alice F. Stuhlmacher, Maryalice Citera, and Toni Willis, "Gender Differences in Virtual Negotiation: Theory and Research." *Sex Roles* 57, no. 5 (August 2007): 329–39.

68 **women negotiate against men:** Karin Hederos Eriksson and Anna Sandberg, "Gender Differences in the Initiation of Negotiation: Does the Gender of the Negotiation Counterpart Matter?" *Negotiation Journal* 28, no. 4 (October 2012): 407–28.

Notes

68 **when female athletes negotiate:** Sharon R. Guthrie et al., "Female Athletes Do Ask! An Exploratory Study of Gender Differences in the Propensity to Initiate Negotiation Among Athletes." *Women in Sport and Physical Activity Journal* 18, no. 1 (2009): 90–101.

68–9 **matriarchal versus patriarchal communities:** Steffen Andersen et al., "On the Cultural Basis of Gender Differences in Negotiation." *Experimental Economics* 21, no. 4 (2018): 757–78.

69 **eyebrow-raising study:** Julia Bear and Linda Babcock, "Negotiation Topic as a Moderator of Gender Differences in Negotiation." *Psychological Science* 23, no. 7 (June 2012): 743–44.

69 **13.9 per cent less:** Australian Government/Workplace Gender Equality Agency, "Australia's Gender Pay Gap Statistics." *WGEA,* February 20, 2020.

69 **women were a fourth less likely:** Benjamin Artz, Amanda H. Godall, and Andrew J. Oswald, "Do Women Ask?" *Industrial Relations* 57, no. 4 (October 2018): 611–36.

70 **5.5 times greater for women:** H. R. Bowles et al., "Social Incentives for Gender Differences in the Propensity to Initiate Negotiations: Sometimes It Does Hurt to Ask." *Organizational Behavior and Human Decision Processes* 103, no. 1 (May 2007): 84–103.

70–1 **Nadella issued a statement:** Selena Larson, "Microsoft CEO Satya Nadella Eats Humble Pie Over Remarks to Women." *ReadWrite,* October 8, 2014.

71 **Nadella encouraged women:** Ian Sherr and Connie Guglielmo, "This Is Not Your Father's Microsoft." *CNET,* August 30, 2018.

72 **girls and boys ask about a hundred questions a day:** Po Bronson and Ashley Merryman, "The Creativity Crisis." *Newsweek,* July 10, 2010.

72 **asking questions is good:** Michelle Marie Chouinard, "Children's Questions: A Mechanism for Cognitive Development." *Monographs of the Society for Research in Child Development* 72, no. 1 (March 2007).

72 **stops by middle school:** Bronson and Merryman, "The Creativity Crisis."

Notes

73 **"the answer, not for asking a good question":** "TED Founder Richard Saul Wurman: It's the Question, Not the Answer." YouTube, March 20, 2014; https://www.youtube.com/watch?v=0SekW4Cp1Ks.

74 **experience in negotiating significantly helps women:** Alfred Zerres et al., "Does It Take Two to Tango? Longitudinal Effects of Unilateral and Bilateral Integrative Negotiation Training." *Journal of Applied Psychology* 98, no. 3 (April 2013): 478–91.

77 **apt to ask when they're advocating on behalf of someone:** Vivian Siegel, "Self-Advocacy: Why It's Uncomfortable, Especially for Women, and What to Do About It." *American Society for Cell Biology*, November 7, 2016.

80 **countries that have had equal pay legislation:** Solomon W. Polachek, "Equal Pay Legislation and the Gender Wage Gap." *IZA World of Labor* 16 (2019).

82 **even those who are underqualified:** Nancy F. Clark, "Act Now to Shrink the Confidence Gap." *Forbes,* April 28, 2014.

Chapter 3. Cultivate Her Competitive Spirit

94 **arouses a competitive instinct:** Norman Triplett, "The Dynamogenic Factors in Pacemaking and Competition." *American Journal of Psychology* 9, no. 4 (1898): 507–33.

95 **"the desire to beat":** Triplett, "The Dynamogenic Factors in Pacemaking and Competition."

95 **describe in their book:** Po Bronson and Ashley Merryman, *Top Dog: The Science of Winning and Losing* (New York: Twelve, 2013).

97 **fun but competitive game:** Jan L. Plass et al., "The Impact of Individual, Competitive, and Collaborative Mathematics Game Play on Learning, Performance, and Motivation." *Journal of Educational Psychology* 105, no. 4 (November 2013): 1050–66.

98 **more than 11,750 logo submissions:** Daniel P. Gross, "Creativity Under Fire: The Effects of Competition on Creative Production." Harvard Business School Working Paper 16-109 (March 2016); also author correspondence with Daniel Gross, September 30, 2018.

98 **into untested territory:** Regina Conti, Mary Ann Collins, and Martha L. Picariello, "The Impact of Competition on Intrinsic

Notes

Motivation and Creativity: Considering Gender, Gender Segregation, and Gender Role Orientation." *Personality and Individual Differences* 31, no. 8 (December 2001): 1273–89.

100 **approximately 90 per cent of the women:** Mandy Dorn, "Ernst & Young Global Survey Reveals Critical Role Sports Play for Female Executives in Leadership Development and Teamwork in Business." *PRWeb,* June 18, 2013; https://www.prweb.com/releases/2013/6 /prweb10841451.htm.

100 **94 percent among women in the most senior:** EY and espnW, "Why Female Athletes Make Winning Entrepreneurs." EY, 2017; https:// assets.ey.com/content/dam/ey-sites/ey-com/en_gl/topics/entrepre neurship/ey-why-female-athletes-make-winning-entrepreneurs.pdf.

101 **74 per cent of female executives:** "Female executives say participation in sport helps accelerate leadership and career potential." ESPN, October 9, 2014; https://espnpressroom.com/us/press-releases/2014 /10/female-executives-say-participation-in-sport-helps-accelerate -leadership-and-career-potential/

102 **"a strong negative effect on women's interest":** Jessica Preece and Olga Stoddard, "Why Women Don't Run: Experimental Evidence on Gender Differences in Political Competition Aversion." *Journal of Economic Behavior & Organization* 117 (September 2015): 296–308.

102 **subject of scrutiny:** Brad Barber, "Gender Differences in Investing: Shifting the Financial Services Industry." UC Davis, April 23, 2012; https://gsm.ucdavis.edu/blog/gender-differences-investing.

102 **"I often think about my professional life like a game":** Personal interview with Adrienne Harris, October 2018.

104 **women simply don't like to compete:** Muriel Niederle and Lise Vesterlund, "Do Women Shy Away from Competition? Do Men Compete Too Much?" *Quarterly Journal of Economics* 122, no. 3 (August 2007): 1067–101.

105 **competitiveness in matriarchal versus patriarchal:** Uri Gneezy, Kenneth L. Leonard, and John A. List, "Gender Differences in Competition: Evidence from a Matrilineal and a Patriarchal Society." *Econometrica* 77, no. 5 (September 2009): 1637–64.

Notes

106 **no difference across gender or culture:** Gneezy, Leonard, and List, "Gender Differences in Competition." *Econometrica* 77, no 5 (September 2009): 1637–1664.

107 **fifty pence per maze:** Alison L. Booth and Patrick J. Nolen, "Choosing to Compete: How Different Are Girls and Boys?" *IZA Discussion Papers 4027,* February 2009.

116 **library hosts a junior author contest:** "Poetry Contest Winners." *Lower Merion Library System,* last modified April 16, 2019.

118 **athletes are shown to perform better:** Gwendolyn Perry-Burney and Baffour Takyi, "Self Esteem, Academic Achievement, and Moral Development Among Adolescent Girls." *Journal of Human Behavior in the Social Environment* 5, no. 2 (March 2002): 15–27.

118 **girls stop playing competitive sports twice as often:** "Factors Influencing Girls' Participation in Sports." *Women's Sports Foundation,* September 9, 2016.

118 **over 50 per cent of teenage girls:** Jolie Egan, "Half of Girls Quit Sports by the End of Puberty." *Business Wire,* June 28, 2016.

120 **"Winning isn't everything, but wanting to win is":** This well-known quote originated with Henry "Red" Sanders, a college football coach, though it is also often attributed to Vince Lombardi, professional football player and coach.

Chapter 4. Nurture Her Collaborative Problem-Solving Skills

129 **practise collaborating on real-world problems:** "The Interview: Jaime Casap, Education Evangelist at Google." Reimagine Education; https://www.reimagine-education.com/28-jaime-casap-interview/.

129 **"more than just knowledge and skills":** "Definition and Selection of Competencies." OECD Definition and Selection of Competencies website, May 27, 2005, 4.

129 **dental schools have started shifting:** Laura J. Mueller-Joseph and Luisa Nappo-Dattoma, "Collaborative Learning in Pre-Clinical Dental Hygiene Education." *Journal of Dental Hygiene* 87, no. 2 (April 2013): 64–72.

130 **bridge the gap between university and the actual practice of law:** Philippa Ryan, "Teaching Collaborative Problem-Solving Skills to Law Students." *The Law Teacher* 51, no. 2 (2017): 138–50.

Notes

134 **"many ways to screw the pooch":** Margot Lee Shetterly, *Hidden Figures: The American Dream and the Untold Story of the Black Women Mathematicians Who Helped Win the Space Race* (New York: William Morrow 2016), 214.

134 **biggest hurdles for America's race to the moon:** Joel Achenbach, "How Did NASA Put Men on the Moon? One Harrowing Step at a Time." *Washington Post*, June 19, 2019; https://www.washingtonpost. com/national/2019/06/19/how-did-nasa-put-men-moon-one -harrowing-step-time.

135 **"turn their desks into a trigonometric war room":** Shetterly, *Hidden Figures*, 189.

135 **"Here in space":** Video message from Jessica Meir to the Baldwin School from International Space Station, February 24, 2020.

136 **"Expeditionary Skills for Life":** "Lesson Plan: Activity 1.1." NASA; https://www.nasa.gov/sites/default/files/atoms/files/esfl_es_pipe line.pdf.

137 **"monitoring progress towards a solution":** Briony Harris, "Girls Are Better Than Boys at Solving Problems in Teams, Especially in These Countries." World Economic Forum, January 16, 2018.

137 **"top performers" at this essential twenty-first-century skill:** *PISA 2015 Results (Volume V): Collaborative Problem Solving* (Paris: OECD Publishing, 2017).

137 **gender gap is even larger than for reading:** Harris, "Girls Are Better."

138 **"better equipped for the workplace":** Harris, "Girls Are Better."

139 **eighty four- and five-year-olds were divided:** William R. Charlesworth and Claire Dzur, "Gender Comparisons of Preschoolers' Behavior and Resource Utilization in Group Problem Solving." *Child Development* 58, no. 1 (1987): 191–200.

140 **verbal communication skills to find compromises:** Heather A. Holmes-Lonergan, "Preschool Children's Collaborative ProblemSolving Interactions: The Role of Gender, Pair Type, and Task." *Sex Roles* 48, no. 11 (June 2003): 505–17.

141 **solve the problem without collaborating at all:** Holmes-Lonergan, "Preschool Children's Collaborative Problem-Solving Interactions."

Notes

141 **prescriptive gender stereotypes:** Anne M. Koenig, "Comparing Prescriptive and Descriptive Gender Stereotypes About Children, Adults, and the Elderly." *Frontiers in Psychology* 9 (2018); https://doi .org/10.3389/fpsyg.2018.01086.

141 **group norms that unconsciously influence:** Eleanor E. Maccoby, *The Two Sexes: Growing Up Apart, Coming Together* (Cambridge, MA: Belknap Press, 1998).

141 **how young girls and boys interact with peers:** Richard A. Fabes, Carol Lynn Martin, and Laura D. Hanish, "Young children's play qualities in same-, other-, and mixed-sex peer groups." *Child Development* 74, no. 3 (May 2003): 921–32.

141 **how friends influence:** Amanda J. Rose and Karen D. Rudolph, "A Review of Sex Differences in Peer Relationship Processes: Potential Trade-offs for the Emotional and Behavioral Development of Girls and Boys." *Psychological Bulletin* 132, no. 1 (January 2006): 98–131.

141 **likely to prioritize mutually beneficial outcomes:** JoNell Strough and Cynthia A. Berg, "Goals as a Mediator of Gender Differences in High-Affiliation Dyadic Conversations." *Developmental Psychology* 36, no. 1 (January 2000): 117–25.

142 **women represent 22 per cent:** "Women in Peacekeeping," UN Peacekeeping; https://peacekeeping.un.org/en/women-peacekeeping.

142 **how influential women are for modern peacekeeping:** Elisabeth Porter, "Women, Political Decision-Making, and Peace-Building." *Global Change, Peace & Security* 15, no. 3 (October 2003): 245–62.

145 **as many as six percentage points:** *PISA 2015 Results*, 40.

146 **a more diverse peer group helps children:** *PISA 2015 Results*, 43.

147 **higher scores in their ability to effectively problem-solve:** Jeffery Mo, "What Kinds of Activities Are Common Among Teenagers Who Work Well with Others?" *PISA in Focus*, no. 84 (2018).

147 **who generally exhibit more perfectionistic:** Claire Shipman, Katty Kay, and JillEllyn Riley, "How Puberty Kills Girls' Confidence." *The Atlantic*, September 20, 2018.

147 **risk-aversive tendencies:** Lauren B. Alloy et al., "Pubertal Development, Emotion Regulatory Styles, and the Emergence of Sex

Differences in Internalizing Disorders and Symptoms in Adolescence." *Clinical Psychological Science* 4, no. 5 (September 2016): 867–81.

147 **part of the process and of the fun:** Cara Masset, "Risky Thinking." *Carnegie Mellon Today,* March 14, 2016; https://www.cmu.edu/cmtoday/science_innovation/cognitive-psychology-of-risk-taking/index.html.

148 **study that investigated collaborative problem-solving:** *PISA 2015 Results.*

149 **massively multiplayer online role-playing games:** Constance Steinkuehler, "Massively Multiplayer Online Games as an Educational Technology: An Outline for Research." *Educational Technology* 48, no. 1 (January–February 2008): 10–21.

149 **fun ways to work on this important skill:** Ya-Ting Carolyn Yang, "Building Virtual Cities, Inspiring Intelligent Citizens: Digital Games for Developing Students' Problem Solving and Learning Motivation." *Computers & Education* 59, no. 2 (September 2012): 365–77.

Chapter 5. Make Empathy Her Natural Advantage

160 **"ability to understand another person's perspective":** Daniel Goleman, "What Is Empathy?" in *Empathy, HBR Emotional Intelligence Series* (Cambridge, MA: Harvard Business Review Press, 2017).

161 **"influence others in your organization":** Adam Waytz, "The Limits of Empathy." *Harvard Business Review,* January–February 2016, 68–73. For other research on the impact of empathy in daily life, see Annie McKee, "Empathy Is Key to a Great Meeting." *Harvard Business Review,* March 23, 2015.

161 **empathy is positively correlated:** William A. Gentry, Todd J. Weber, and Golnaz Sadri, "Empathy in the Workplace: A Tool for Effective Leadership." *Center for Creative Leadership White Paper,* April 2007.

161 **"empathy tops the list":** Evan Sinar, Ph.D, Rich Wellins, Ph.D., Matthew Paese, Ph.D., Audrey Smith, Ph.D., Bruce Watt, Ph.D., "Is Empathy Boss?" *Development Dimensions International,* 2016, 20–23.

161 **tech companies like Microsoft:** Michal Lev-Ram, "Microsoft CEO Satya Nadella Says Empathy Makes You a Better Innovator." *Fortune,* October 3, 2017.

Notes

161 **companies like the snack maker KIND:** Ashoka, "Meet the CEO Who Is Championing Kindness and Whose Company Runs On It." *Forbes,* February 17, 2016.

161–62 **medical leaders like the Cleveland Clinic:** Tom Sullivan, "Cleveland Clinic CEO: Time to Rethink How We Communicate for Empathy." *Healthcare IT News,* May 14, 2019.

162 **Warby Parker's success:** Dani Clanaman, "Warby Parker's 7 Lessons for New Grads." *Wharton Social Impact Initiative,* July 6, 2015.

162 **"I want our managers to care deeply about the people who work for them":** Leigh Buchanan, "Warby Parker CEO: Why Empathy Matters." *Inc.,* June 2013.

162 **approximately 20 per cent of U.S. employers:** Joann S. Lublin, "Companies Try a New Strategy: Empathy Training." *Wall Street Journal,* June 21, 2016.

163 **typical ergonomic challenges facing pregnant women:** Lublin, "Companies Try a New Strategy"; Jim Mateja, "Ford Engineers Design with Comfort in Mind." *Los Angeles Times,* August 6, 2003.

163 **line of toys designed for girls:** Bernard Garrette, Corey Phelps, and Olivier Sibony, *Cracked It!: How to Solve Big Problems and Sell Solutions Like Top Strategy Consultants* (New York: Palgrave Macmillan, 2018), 154–56.

164 **American military officials decided to incorporate empathy training:** Department of the Army, "FM 6-22 Leader Development Field Manual." Army Publishing Directorate, June 30, 2015.

164 **"empathy is essential to success on and off the battlefield":** Personal correspondence with H. R. McMaster, February 8, 2020.

167 **48 per cent decrease:** Sarah Konrath, Edward O'Brien, and Courtney Hsing, "Changes in Dispositional Empathy in American College Students Over Time: A Meta-Analysis." *Personality and Social Psychology Review* 15, no. 2 (2011): 180–98.

167 **increased levels of individualism:** Jean M. Twenge, "The Duality of Individualism: Attitudes Toward Women, Generation Me, and

Notes

the Method of Cross-Temporal Meta-Analysis." *Psychology of Women Quarterly* 35, no. 1 (March 2011): 193–96.

167 **and increased materialism:** Juliet B. Schor, *Born to Buy: The Commercialized Child and the New Consumer Culture* (New York: Scribner, 2005).

167 **correlates to weaker personal relationships:** Kathleen D. Vohs, Nicole L. Mead, and Miranda R. Goode. "The Psychological Consequences of Money." *Science* 314, no. 5802 (2006): 1154–56.

167 **"hard-wired for empathy":** Simon Baron-Cohen, *The Essential Difference: The Truth About the Male and Female Brain* (New York: Basic Books, 2003), 1.

168 **different empathetic skills within the first year of life:** Erin B. McClure, "A Meta-Analytic Review of Sex Differences in Facial Expression Processing and Their Development in Infants, Children, and Adolescents." *Psychological Bulletin* 126, no. 3 (May 2000): 424–53; Megan R. Gunnar and Margaret Donahue, "Sex Differences in Social Responsiveness Between Six Months and Twelve Months." *Child Development* 51, no. 1 (March 1980): 262–65.

168 **"How did the Rodney cartoon make you feel at the end?":** Ruth Zajdel et al., "Children's Understanding and Experience of Mixed Emotions: The Roles of Age, Gender, and Empathy." *Journal of Genetic Psychology* 174, no. 5 (March 2013): 582–603.

169 **perceptions of their empathetic ability:** Mathias Allemand, Andrea Steiger, and Helmut Fend, "Empathy Development in Adolescence Predicts Social Competencies in Adulthood." *Journal of Personality* 83, no. 2 (April 2015): 229–41.

169 **empathy among undergraduate medical students:** Marta Duarte, Mario Raposo, and Miguel Castelo-Branco, "Measuring Empathy in Medical Students, Gender Differences and Level of Medical Education." *Investigación en Educación Médica* 5, no. 20 (October–December 2016): 253–60.

170 **gendered perceptions of altruistic behaviour:** Hiromi Taniguchi, "Men's and Women's Volunteering: Gender Differences in the Effects

Notes

of Employment and Family Characteristics." *Nonprofit and Voluntary Sector Quarterly* 35, no. 1 (March 2006): 83–101.

170 **"come to the aid of others":** Leonardo Christov-Moore et al., "Empathy: Gender Effects in Brain and Behavior." *Neuroscience & Biobehavioral Reviews* 46, no. 4 (October 2014): 604–27.

170 **80 per cent of Americans:** Paul Taylor, "Court of Public Opinion Sides with Women on Empathy." Pew Research Center, May 21, 2009; https://www.pewresearch.org/2009/05/21/court-of-public-opinion-sides-with-women-on-empathy/.

171 **women were "nurturing and empathetic":** Kim Parker, Juliana Menasce Horowitz, and Renee Stepler, "Americans See Different Expectations for Men and Women." Pew Research Center, December 5, 2017; https://www.pewsocialtrends.org/2017/12/05/americans-see-different-expectations-for-men-and-women/.

171 **33 to 50 per cent of a toddler's empathetic behaviour:** Ariel Knafo et al. "The Developmental Origins of a Disposition Toward Empathy: Genetic and Environmental Contributions." *Emotion* 8, no. 6 (December 2008): 737–52.

172 **you get an empathic child by:** Roman Krznaric, *Empathy: Why It Matters, and How to Get It* (New York: Perigee, 2014).

174 **empathetic accuracy:** William Ickes, ed., *Empathic Accuracy* (New York: Guilford Press, 1997), 2.

175 **reading narrative fiction:** Raymond A. Mar, Keith Oatley, and Jordan B. Peterson, "Exploring the Link Between Reading Fiction and Empathy: Ruling Out Individual Differences and Examining Outcomes." *Communications* 34 (December 2009): 407–28.

175 **abilities to infer what other people are thinking:** P. Matthijs Bal and Martijn Veltkamp, "How Does Fiction Reading Influence Empathy? An Experimental Investigation on the Role of Emotional Transportation." *PLoS One* 8, no. 1 (January 30, 2013).

176 **"potential to experience empathetic sensibility":** Krznaric, *Empathy*, 152.

177 **getting involved in service projects helps:** Marie L. Masterson and Katharine C. Kersey, "Connecting Children to Kindness: Encour-

Notes

aging a Culture of Empathy." *Childhood Education* 89, no. 4 (July 2013): 211–16.

Chapter 6. Her Ability to Adapt Will Be Key

184 **leaving Flywheel and life in the corporate world:** Elyse Steinhaus, "An Exec Who Spent 20 Years Working for Companies Like Virgin Atlantic and Nike Explains How She Kept from Being Boxed into a Single Industry." *Business Insider,* November 29, 2016.

184 **"It's the obstacles that help me":** Personal conversation with Sarah Robb O'Hagan, June 25, 2019, and interview for Tory Burch Foundation; http://www.toryburchfoundation.org/resources/growth/sarah -robb-ohagan/.

187 **"adapting to new problems":** Personal communication with Kate Kohler Shattuck, December 16, 2019.

189 **"ability to modify or adjust one's behaviour":** Gary Roger Vanden-Bos, *APA Dictionary of Psychology,* 2nd ed. (Washington, DC: American Psychological Association, 2015), 18.

189 **drivers of personal and professional success:** Lee J. Miller and Wei Lu, "Gen Z Is Set to Outnumber Millennials Within a Year." *Bloomberg,* August 20, 2018.

190 **Fourth Industrial Revolution:** Klaus Schwab, *The Fourth Industrial Revolution* (New York: Currency, 2017).

190 **65 per cent of the jobs:** "The Future of Jobs: Employment, Skills and Workforce Strategy for the Fourth Industrial Revolution." *World Economic Forum Global Challenge Insight Report,* January 2016.

190 **phenomena like the gig economy:** A. J. Brustein, "Data on the Gig Economy and How It Is Transforming the Workforce." Wonolo, February 15, 2018; https://www.wonolo.com/blog/data-gig-economy -transforming-workforce.

190 **likely to change jobs more often:** "Employee Tenure Summary." U.S. Bureau of Labor Statistics, September 20, 2018; https://www. bls.gov/news.release/pdf/tenure.pdf.

Notes

191 **"ability to adapt to change":** "Accelerating the Pace and Impact of Digital Transformation." *Harvard Business Review Analytic Services Report,* 2016.

191 **"must become our central competency":** Gen. Stanley McChrystal et al., *Team of Teams: New Rules of Engagement for a Complex World* (New York: Portfolio, 2015), 20.

192 **"technological advancements that we have no idea are coming":** Personal communication with Kate Kohler Shattuck, December 16, 2019.

192 **drivers of a person's adaptability:** Stu Crandell, Joy Hazucha, and J. Evelyn Orr, "Precision Talent Intelligence: The Definitive Four Dimensions of Leadership and Talent." *Korn Ferry Institute,* 2014.

192 **mothers are entering the workforce:** Women's Bureau, U.S. Department of Labor, "Mothers and Families," 2017.

194 **"You have to adapt to all of that":** Personal interview with Margie Cohn, December 11, 2019.

196 **stories from people holding twenty-one different:** Elaine D. Pulakos et al., "Adaptability in the Workplace: Development of a Taxonomy of Adaptive Performance." *Journal of Applied Psychology* 85, no. 4 (August 2000): 612–24.

197 **969 students from middle and senior schools:** A. J. Martin et al., "Adaptability: How Students' Responses to Uncertainty and Novelty Predict Their Academic and Non-Academic Outcomes." *Journal of Educational Psychology* 105, no. 3 (August 2013): 728–46; Andrew Martin, "Coping with Change: Teaching Adaptability Will Help Kids Grow," *The Conversation,* November 10, 2013.

201 **adaptive performance can also be nurtured:** Jeffery LePine, Jason Colquitt, and Amir Erez, "Adaptability to Changing Task Contexts: Effects of General Cognitive Ability, Conscientiousness, and Openness to Experience." *Personnel Psychology* 53, no. 3 (December 2006): 563–93.

202 **readily fostered in both kids and adults:** Emma C. Burns, Andrew J. Martin, and Rebecca J. Collie, "Adaptability, Personal Best (PB) Goals Setting, and Gains in Students' Academic Outcomes: A

Notes

Longitudinal Examination from a Social Cognitive Perspective." *Contemporary Educational Psychology* 53 (April 2018): 57–72.

205 growth mindset and resilience: Christine Gross-Low, "How Praise Became a Consolation Prize," *The Atlantic,* December 16, 2016; Angela Duckworth, *Grit: The Power of Passion and Perseverance* (New York: Scribner, 2016). See also Reshma Saujani, *Brave, Not Perfect: Fear Less, Fail More, and Live Bolder* (New York: Currency, 2019).

205 storytelling helps improve: Wendy Joung, Beryl Hesketh, and Andrew Neal, "Using War Stories to Train for Adaptive Performance: Is It Better to Learn from Error or Success?" *Applied Psychology* 55, no. 2 (April 2006): 282–302.